HOLY SPIRIT VINDICATION

RIGHT
REASONABLE
JUSTIFIED

TODD MOZINGO

You may contact Pastor Mozingo through his church website:
https://reviveusnow.com

Editors: June Dunai, Jan Mozingo, Paul Garner
Graphics: Mariah Camacho

DEDICATION

I would like to dedicate this book first and foremost to my wife Jan who has worked tirelessly with me through this work God has given us to do. Next, I want to recognize my two awesome daughters, Brianne and Brittney who I am forever proud of for putting up with me while becoming wonderful women of God. Finally, I dedicate this book to all of those who have gone with us on this journey of vindicating the Holy Spirit. Those who stayed with us as we took a stand to ensure that the Holy Spirit was recognized, loved and followed in the church today!

ENDORSEMENTS

Straight up teaching that the church today needs to hear! It's time for the Holy Spirit and the Word of God to come back together in the church and Pastor Todd clearly explains what that can mean for believers today.

R.T. Kendall
Author of over sixty books
Former Senior Minister, Westminster Chapel, London

This book speaks strongly to a problematic issue in the church throughout the world. The third Person of the Trinity is generally feared. In many churches, substituting a costly twisted identity which reads, God the Father, God the Son and God the Holy Bible, resulting in a weakness which is all too obvious. The Holy Spirit within each of us is absolutely indispensable and necessary and marks the powerful and revelatory feature that sets Christianity apart from every religion on earth. The source of power for the effectiveness of every Christian and the church, in general is in the Holy Spirit alone. The Church may influence the world with truth but without the Holy Spirit there is no power. We are here not only to speak the truth but to trust the Holy Spirit for transformation power.
This author has spoken effectively from experience, declaring, defending and defining the full work of the Spirit of God, having experienced personally in his own life as well as in the church which he so effectively leads.

Reading and applying these truths so powerfully set forth here will not only meet our inner needs but will render us as powerful agents in personal ministry everywhere we go! Well done, Todd!

Jack R. Taylor, President
Dimensions Ministries
Melbourne, Florida

Todd Mozingo demands a change. The book you now hold, Holy Spirit Vindication, will open your eyes to the ongoing work God has entrusted to you. Study the message, believe it, enforce it. A new life awaits you in the pages you hold. Go for it!

Charles Carrin
Charles Carrin Ministries
Boynton Beach, Florida

CONTENTS

HOLY SPIRIT INTRODUCTION

What is happening to the church? Is our experience in the church today what God intended? Is the goal of Christianity to be good, moralistic people who feed the hungry and give out Christmas presents, leaving us feeling we are doing the work of God? Why are we here? What is our purpose? And what are we supposed to be doing?

I grew up in a conservative, traditional, Bible-based church. We believed that if it was not in scripture, then you did not do it. We spoke where the Bible speaks and were silent where the Bible was silent. We went to church gatherings several times per week, helped each other out, sent money to missionaries and believed that we were doing exactly what we were supposed to be doing. Sometimes we lacked excitement and passion, but we were faithful. And at the same time, many of the things that are in scripture never seemed to happen for us. The scripture was full of the miraculous–of healing and deliverance, of amazing, exciting, and supernatural things. We seemed content with just being nice people while we waited for Jesus to come and take us to heaven.

There were other churches that were very different from the one I grew up in. Most people referred to them as 'charismatic' or 'Spirit-filled'. They seemed to think that church was about having an experience. They were dynamic and emotional. They believed in the miraculous, but for me they had a peculiar way of pursuing it. They seemed to care more about "what could happen". They were constantly looking for something they called revival. They wanted it, but pursued it with things that did not make sense to me. And they were definitely doing things that did not seem to be in the bible–certainly not things I had learned.

There is an obvious polarization between these types of churches. The conservative group said the charismatic group did not adhere to the Bible. The charismatic group said the conservative group rejected the things that were in the Bible. Both groups seemed to believe they had it right and the other did not.

But why the difference if we are reading the same instruction manual?

How could the church be so different if we are all serving the same God? What was God's intent for the church today? It seems obvious that we all want to fulfill God's plan for our lives and for the church, so maybe it's time to take a closer look.

Years after being called into ministry, something happened to me. I had an experience with the Holy Spirit that changed everything. It completely flipped my views of why the church exists today. I began to see who we are supposed to be as the church. Things were missing in both the conservative and the charismatic churches. Maybe through years of defending what we believe, we have lost a focus that we need to reclaim.

In John 16, Jesus left the earth to return to the throne of God. In doing so, He told us that we were to be led by the Holy Spirit. But what does that mean? What has happened to the role of the Holy Spirit in our churches today? Are we being led by the Spirit in a biblical way? Is the Holy Spirit just someone who provides an emotional experience, or does He have another purpose? Does the Holy Spirit have the role in the church today that God designed for us or have we defined his role in some other way that seems to work better for us? Is it possible that the Holy Spirit had a role in the early church that we don't give him today? And if that is true, would we want to know what it is?

For any one of us, if we have been falsely accused, if there is misinformation spread about us, if people have been deceived about who we are, we want vindication! Maybe, in the church today, the Holy Spirit needs vindication.

HOLY SPIRIT VINDICATION

You may live in an area or territory that is saturated with the presence of the Holy Spirit, but most people do not. Even territories with thriving Spirit-filled churches have dry areas around them and are looking for more. No doubt, many parts of the country and world are crying out desperately for a move of the Holy Spirit. In the area where I live, if we look at the well known Spirit-filled churches that have been in this area over just the last 40 years, although several have been here, maybe one remains. There has not been a strong presence of Spirit-filled churches in this area praying and crying out for revival for quite some time. Over the last several decades several have, but they have not lasted.

Of the Spirit-filled churches that have been in this area, some have exploded in growth only to quickly shrink back in size–one grew to 700 people and just as quickly dissolved to nothing. Another grew to 400, then shrank back down to 40. What I believe has been going on is that there has been attack on the Holy Spirit in our territory. I believe there has been a silencing by the enemy of the Holy Spirit in this area and in many other areas as well. I believe Christianity is strong in our territory, but it's mostly without the presence of a powerful Holy Spirit. I believe this may be true for where you live as well. Please know that, as I discuss this and dive into this issue in more detail, I'm not disrespecting any other churches in any area. I'm not going through their statements of faith. I'm not making any judgments on them or what they believe, but what I do not see is a major presence of the Holy Spirit moving in churches today. I believe as you read this, you may find it applies to your area as well.

Instead, what I see are moralistic people, good people, giving people, people who care about others, but people operating without power! Again, let me remind you, I'm not condemning, that's not my intention. The scripture says that signs, wonders and miracles are supposed to follow believers. Let me explain what I mean by that. I think signs, wonders and miracles occur anytime the spiritual realm affects or creates a change in the physical realm. When that happens, it falls in the category of signs, wonders and miracles. Things like instant healing, the casting out of demons, speaking in tongues with interpretation, visions, prophetic speech, and other manifestations are common and normal when the spiritual realm affects the physical realm. But let's look at this scripture before we get into it.

In Mark 16:15-18, Jesus is speaking, and He said to them:

> Go into all the world and preach the gospel to all creation. He who has believed and has been baptized shall be saved; but he who has disbelief shall be condemned. These signs will accompany those who have believed: In My name they will cast out demons, they will speak in new tongues; they will pick up serpents and if they drink any deadly poison, it will not hurt them; they will lay hands on the sick and they will recover.

Now to make this very clear, we do NOT chase signs, wonders and miracles! We do not chase these, BUT because of our belief, signs, wonders and miracles chase us! Can you see this? It's an indication that the two work together! If there is a substantial belief, and it's who we're called to be, and the power of the Spirit is working through us and moving in us, then signs, wonders and miracles will follow us. It just happens–it's how it works in The Kingdom, AND it's what The Word says!

In other words, these gifts will be present because there are believers who believe so strongly in the Kingdom of God and the presence of the Holy Spirit that those things HAVE to manifest! But some people have asked me: “Should we be praying for signs, wonders, and miracles? Isn't that kind of chasing them?”

To answer this, let's look at the Apostle’s prayer in Acts 4:29-31:

> And now Lord, take note of their threats, *(talking about the ones coming against them)*, and grant that Your bond servants may speak the word with all confidence, while you extend Your hand to heal, and signs and wonders take place through the name of Your holy servant Jesus. And when they had prayed, the place where they were gathered together began to shake and they were all filled with the Holy Spirit and began to speak the word of God with boldness.

They were praying that, if we could speak with boldness and confidence, then your hand Lord, would come and perform the signs, the wonders, and miracles.

As a pastor, I also don't want to be remiss in the warning that Jesus gives in Matthew 24:24:

> For false Christs and false prophets will arise, and they will show great signs and wonders so as to mislead, if possible, even the elect.

So we must use wisdom and our knowledge of scripture. It’s imperative that we use spiritual discernment to be open to what the Spirit is doing and wants to do–just as much as what could be false. I grew up in a place that taught, ‘If it's not in the Bible, it can't happen. It's not of God’. Therefore we must also fully examine the Word of God, the Scripture, the baseline and plumb line that we follow.

I fully believe that if it's in the Word of God, it's possible and probable for us today! But are we limited to what is written in scripture only? Do you remember what happened on the day of Pentecost with Peter and the apostles in the upper room, when a rushing wind comes, and tongues of fire land on every one of their heads? Should Peter have said, “Wait a minute, that's not in the Torah! I've never heard or read of fire falling on individual people's heads. This can't be of God! It must be demonic. Okay, we better run and get out of here?” What? They were totally in God's presence, and now we are to believe that suddenly the enemy has shown up to deceive them? No! Here’s the difference: They knew the character of

God. They knew the presence of God. They had discernment in the Spirit, so they knew this was of God. They knew that this was a move of the Spirit because they knew the Spirit. They had received the Spirit in John 20, over 40 days before the day of Pentecost. So, it's not about the legalities of scripture, it's about the application of scripture. Is it possible that if we don't know the Spirit of God, we might not be open to a move of His Spirit?

Sobering, isn't it?

So, what is the point?

We need to know the character of God!

If we are in the Spirit, we can discern the false from the real.

Matthew 24:24 says:

> For false Christs and false prophets will arise and will show great signs and wonders so as to mislead, if possible, even the elect.

So how do we ensure that this will not happen to us? We must know the Spirit. We must learn how to discern things in the Spirit. We must know the truth of the Word, and we will not be deceived. We are equipped by the Spirit to identify a false work, and in contrast, a move of the Spirit.

I believe it's time we take back our territories! Even in the area where we have been planted, I am confident that we are here for the Holy Spirit to be vindicated.

But what do I mean by this?

Here's the definition of vindication. Vindication is proof that someone or something is right, reasonable and justified. In other words, how does the Holy Spirit become right, reasonable and justified in a territory, especially in an area where He has been ushered out, ignored or rejected?

What does this vindication look like, and how would we get there? What would a church that welcomes and vindicates the Holy Spirit in a territory look like? We want to look biblically at what happens when the Holy Spirit is moving in the church and has the freedom to not be silenced. We can see in scripture what it looks like when the Holy Spirit is moving. Let's start in one of my favorite chapters, John 16. It is greatly overlooked and often ignored by many believers and a lot of theologians. I've taught on this scripture a lot, but many still miss it–as I had in the past. Even if you've heard and seen it many times, it bears another look.

John 16:8-11 says:

> And He, when He comes, will convict the world concerning sin and righteousness and judgment; concerning sin, because they do not believe in Me; and concerning righteousness, because I go to the Father and you no longer see Me; and concerning judgment, because the ruler of this world has been judged.

Jesus is speaking of the Holy Spirit and He says that when He comes, when the Holy Spirit comes, He will convict the world concerning sin and righteousness and judgment. I know believer, after believer, after believer who thinks the job of the Holy Spirit is to convict me of my sin, convict me to do the right thing, and convict me that there's going to be a judgment one day.

But that's not what this says. Let's read what verse nine says first, 'now concerning sin'. He says, concerning sin, because THEY do not believe in me. In other words, He's talking to the disciples and He says the Holy Spirit is going to convict of sin because THEY don't believe. Read carefully, He did NOT say because you disciples don't believe. He is not talking about the disciples. He says THEY don't believe me. You, disciples, have already believed. You have already been convicted of your sin, that's why you believe. You've accepted the need for a Savior. THEY, the non-believer, is going to be convicted of their sin. That's what the Holy Spirit is coming to do–convict the non-believer of sin.

Then the next statement is: ‘and concerning righteousness, because I go to the Father and YOU no longer see me.’ Here He is addressing the disciples. Jesus says to the disciples that you need to be convicted of your righteousness. Jesus says the reason you need to be convicted of your righteousness is because I am no longer going to be with you to do that. The Holy Spirit will now convict you of your righteousness. I firmly believe this is missing in most Christians’ walk today. We need to be convicted of our righteousness. When we come to a saving knowledge of Christ, the Bible says we are clothed in righteousness–His righteousness. We now have right standing with God. We are righteous in His eyes. We are hidden in Christ. There is therefore now no condemnation for those who are in Christ. Do you see that? The believer needs to be convicted that he is righteous! How would we be different if we realized our righteousness instead of constantly struggling with sinfulness? We would walk through life with grace and have an air in our step when we realize we are not sinners saved by grace. The truth is, we WERE sinners, but we are NOW saved, washed in the blood, cleansed of our impurities by grace, and He calls us righteous before Him! WOW! What a revelation it is to walk from a righteous standpoint!

Finally, He says “and judgment, because the ruler of this world has been judged.” Who is He addressing now? The enemy. That's right–the judgement is for the enemy. The enemy is defeated! He's judged. It is finished, and we are victorious! There are three groups of beings on this planet: the lost, the saved and the demonic. Jesus says the Holy Spirit will address all three. The lost will be convicted of sin, the saved will be convicted of their righteousness, and the demonic will be convicted of their coming judgment!

What this means for us is, the Holy Spirit didn't come to make us feel bad, to tell us to be good, and to warn us that there is a judgment one day. He came to tell the lost that they need Christ. He came to convict them of their sin. He came to tell believers that we need to be convicted of our righteousness! Can you imagine how we would pray if we knew we were righteous? Can we imagine what would happen in the lives of the church if we acted like righteous people? Let’s look at where the church universal is struggling with this righteousness today. The big question that's moving through the church today is:

“Is it okay to sin since we're under grace?”

The truth is, if we are convicted of our righteousness, we won't be asking that question.

Here is one way to look at it. It would be like being married and saying, “Hey, is it okay if I have affairs on my spouse because she loves me?” That would be absurd! My spouse loves me so much, but this beautiful, unconditional love in no way makes it okay for me to abuse that love and sleep around on my spouse because I'm under my spouse’s love. Right? That wouldn’t make any sense! Why would I have any desire to sleep around when my spouse loves me so much? Why would I take advantage of this beautiful love? It's the same way with Christ! Are we not His bride?

Why and how would we ever do that to him? There's no way that we can live in the Kingdom of God, in the kingdom of light, in the kingdom of love and then say, “I'm going to step over into the kingdom of darkness and it's going to be okay.” If we decide to re-enter the kingdom of darkness, we’ve just created a bridge for the kingdom of darkness and it’s consequences to come back into our lives. Why would we do that? We want to walk in righteousness. Our desire under grace is for more of Jesus, not less of Jesus. When people desire to sin and take advantage of grace, I just want to say, “God help us church, we are an adulterous people!”

The Holy Spirit needs to be vindicated in our lives. If we made Him the priority, we would be a people who are led, taught, and guided into truth by the Holy Spirit. Then the grip of sin would be released from us and we would walk in the righteousness we are intended to walk in.

Next, I believe that if the Holy Spirit were vindicated, we would not be ashamed to say we are led by the Spirit. Let's look at how that plays out, because most Christians will say, I follow Jesus. I follow Christ. We follow Jesus, that's true, but this next point is important. It is the Christ we follow who told us to follow the Holy Spirit. If we look at John 14:26-27 when Jesus is explaining to the disciples about the Holy Spirit, this is what he says:

> But the Helper, the Holy Spirit whom the Father will send in My name, He will teach you all things, and bring to your remembrance all that I said to you.

When we look forward into John 16:12, Jesus says:

> I have many more things to say to you, but you cannot bear them now. But when He, the Spirit of truth, comes, He will guide you into all truth; for He will not speak on His own initiative, but whatever He hears, He will speak, and He will disclose to you what is to come.

Did you see the words of Jesus? "He will teach you"… "He will guide you"… "He will speak"… "He will disclose to you." So, it's Jesus's instruction to us to follow the Holy Spirit. We must understand how the government of the Kingdom of God is set up. Christ has returned to the right hand of the Father, at the throne to take His rightful place there. He has sent the Holy Spirit to us, and He says: "you will now be taught and guided into all truth, by the Holy Spirit." We are led into truth by the Holy Spirit. The Holy Spirit is who we have been instructed to listen to. It's not disrespecting Jesus to follow the Holy Spirit, and it's not disrespecting God. It's what they set up for us! When we follow the lead of the Holy Spirit, we're actually being obedient to Christ. But the converse is also true–if we do not follow the Holy Spirit, we are being disobedient to Christ. That is a bold statement, but re-read these scriptures. It's not semantics–it's obedience!

We need to be taught and guided by the Holy Spirit because Jesus said in John 16:7:

> But I tell you the truth, it is to your advantage that I go away; for if I do not go away, the Helper will not come to you; but if I go, I will send Him to you.

And in John 15:26 Jesus says:

> When the Helper comes, whom I will send to you from the Father, that is the Spirit of truth who proceeds from the Father, He will testify about Me, and you will testify also, because you have been with Me from the beginning.

If we want to learn about Jesus, we've got to learn about Him from the Holy Spirit. Did you get that? Many believers don't know they need to learn about Jesus from the Holy Spirit. It's His role–it's His job. Right now, in this re-capturing of the kingdom of earth for the Kingdom of God, Jesus is at the throne, and He has sent the Spirit to teach us and to guide us. So, the bottom line is this, we'll begin to speak, teach and know the truth because the Holy Spirit is teaching us and guiding us into that truth. Truth is one of the most valuable assets for the believer, and the Holy Spirit will guide us into truth! The truth is, tradition is not always truth–remember the Pharisees? Religion is not always truth–remember the Pharisees? Bible rules are not always the truth when they are misapplied–remember the Pharisees?

> John 17:17 says:
> Sanctify them in the truth; Your word is truth.
>
> John 3:21:
> Truth comes in light, not in darkness.
>
> John 4:24:
> Truth is in the spirit.
>
> John 8:32:
> Truth has freedom and not bondage.

John 8:44:
Truth does not exist in the devil. He is a liar.

John 17:17:
Truth brings sanctification.

The Holy Spirit will be vindicated when we decide to learn truth from the Holy Spirit and be guided by Him.

Now I'm going to shift just a bit, and it's going to sound like I'm talking about the same thing, but I'm not. I believe the Spirit will be vindicated in our territories when we become people who are led by the Spirit. Now, what do I mean?

Romans 8:12-14 says:

> So then, brethren, we are under obligation, not to the flesh, to live according to the flesh, for if you are living according to the flesh, you must die; but if by the Spirit, you are putting to death the deeds of the body, you will live. For all who are being led by the Spirit of God, these are the sons of God.

Now let's look at this. What was the first thing that happened to Jesus at His baptism when the Holy Spirit descended on Him? What is the very first thing scripture tells us? He was 'led' into the desert by the Spirit to be tempted. Even Jesus was led by the Spirit. So here's the actual problem in most churches today. We have become afraid of the Holy Spirit. We're so concerned that someone might get out of control in their emotions. We're so concerned about avoiding the abuses in the name of the Holy Spirit that we've decided it would just be easier to silence Him. We have decided, "Holy Spirit, you make too many problems for us." There are too many issues that will have to be addressed that we are not comfortable with or don't know how to handle, so we just fully squelch the Holy Spirit.

I was with a group of men recently, and a man was telling me about a worship leader that he had been listening to, and the fact that this worship leader was so impactful in her ability to just connect you with the presence of God. Then he said at one point she began singing in tongues while she was leading worship, and instantly, another man in the group said, “Well, that's wrong. That's not in the Bible. You're supposed to have interpretation, or there should be no tongues.” On hearing this, I got up and left the group. I needed to take a minute to calm down. I knew they would look to me for an answer because I'm a pastor, but in the non-Spirit-filled community, and even in the Spirit-filled community, there is a lot of misunderstood doctrine that takes time to re-learn.

What has happened in the church today is that we have eliminated tongues because we don't know how tongues should properly operate in the body, and we have thrown the baby out with the bath water, so to speak. The mentality and improper doctrine that most have in the church is that, if there is no interpreter for one speaking in a tongue, then we should not do it! But we should look in 1 Corinthians 14. We need to look at who is speaking and what he is teaching about tongues. In this chapter, Paul says the following: “do not forbid speaking in tongues.” “I wish you all spoke in tongues.” “I will pray in my spirit and with my mind.” “when you assemble, each one of you has a psalm, a teaching revelation, a tongue.” “If anyone speaks in a tongue, it should be by two or three at the most and there should be an interpreter.” Does that sound like somebody saying we shouldn't be using tongues in church? Not at all. It sounds like somebody who's trying to explain the value of speaking in a different tongue.

What's happened in the church today is that we don't understand the prayer language of tongues that Paul is referencing versus the gift of tongues with interpretation. The first, the prayer language, is meant for personal edification, and the other is meant for the church body. We completely overlook that Paul has an entire explanation of tongues. Then, in verse 19 of chapter 14 he says, “however, in the church.” In other words, here is my explanation of tongues, now let me show how to apply tongues in a church service. He has completely made an explanation and argument FOR tongues and their value before he begins a conversation about using them properly in a church service.

In general, the church doesn't understand the use of tongues as a private prayer language vs. the use of tongues in the church service. Because of this, we make blanket statements regarding the use of tongues at all, just as we do regarding the Holy Spirit in the services. We say, "let's just don't do it, let's just not welcome Him." Of the churches that say "We don't have tongues without interpretation," how many of those churches ever had tongues WITH interpretation? Why not? If they do not have it without interpretation, then why don't they have it with interpretation? It's a valid question!

As believers, do we pray enough in tongues? Are we fully engaged? Are we fulfilling what God has for us with tongues? I don't believe so. If we are discouraged from praying in tongues corporately as a body, we are probably also discouraged from praying in tongues personally, in our private prayer language. Sadly, if we are not led by the Holy Spirit when it comes to the gifts of the Spirit, we will not operate in them either; and tongues are one of the most powerful gifts believers have–SO powerful! We will go deeper and look at a full explanation of tongues in prayer and in the church in a later chapter titled: Holy Spirit–Verbalization.

When the Word of God and the Spirit of God come together, the Spirit is free to move, and the two are balanced because we follow the word and it is applied with the Spirit. When it comes to tongues, we often end up squelching the Holy Spirit due to a lack of understanding. I believe what will happen when there is a vindication of the Spirit is that we will have effective prayer. I don't know of anyone who wouldn't want to have more powerful prayer!

Romans 8:26-27 says:

> In the very same way the Spirit also helps our weakness; for we do not know how to pray as we should, but the Spirit Himself intercedes for US with groanings too deep for words; and He searches the hearts and knows the mind of the Spirit because He intercedes for the saints according to the will of God.

I believe that when we learn who we are in Christ, we will be powerfully praying people. Yes, powerful praying people! Because the same Spirit that raised Jesus from the dead lives in us! The very Creator's Spirit lives in us! The righteous Spirit of God lives in us! The powerful Spirit of God lives in us! The Holy Spirit of God lives in us, and we must positionally understand who we are so that we can properly pray.

The next evidence I see of a vindication of the Spirit is this: the fruits of the Spirit would be evident. We know them!

Galatians 5:22 says:

> The fruit of the Spirit is love, joy, peace, patience, kindness, goodness, faithfulness, gentleness, self-control; and against such things there is no law.

But church, we often don't have the fruit of the Spirit. What we have are the vegetables of the devil: hate, depression, chaos, impatience, rudeness, evil, infidelity, harshness and recklessness. I say this humorously, but how many times have you been to church and what you find is chaos, rude, harsh people, reckless with the things of God. Galatians 5 goes on to say that we should not see these kinds of things in our church: immorality, impurity, sensuality, idolatry, sorcery, enmity, strife, jealousy, outbursts of anger, disputes, dissensions, factions, envying, drunkenness, and carousing. When we look at this list, and when the body of Christ looks at the list, we generally agree these things should not be in the church, things like immorality, idolatry, sorcery, and drunkenness. What if we gave the same amount of attention to disputes, dissension, and factions, because when we remove these things, we have something called unity... UNITY!

So, when the Spirit is vindicated in the church, there will be unity!

Ephesians 4:1-6 says:

> Therefore I, the prisoner of the Lord, implore you to walk in a manner worthy of the calling with which you

> have been called, with all humility and gentleness, with patience, showing tolerance for one another in love, being diligent to preserve the unity of the Spirit in the bond of peace. There is one body, and one Spirit, just as also you were called in one hope of your calling, one Lord, one faith, one baptism, one God and Father of all who is over all and through all and in all.

The church was never meant to be an "each man for himself" kind of place. It was also never meant to be a "my ministry" kind of place. It was never meant to be a "you don't recognize how important I am in the Kingdom of God" kind of place. We shouldn't hear, "My job is to point out what the church is doing wrong." We shouldn't hear, "You need to give me a position so I can have the respect due to me." We shouldn't hear, "This is the way we always did it, so it must be right." What we should hear, and need to hear in the body, is: let's come together with all humility and gentleness, with patience, showing tolerance for one another in love.

Advancing the Kingdom of God is not about us individually. It's about Jesus and His Kingdom!

It's about Jesus, and He is the one who chooses who will lead the local church body. That was His plan when He gave to the church Apostles, Prophets, Teachers, Evangelists and Pastors. We must all be in order and unity, following whomever He chooses to lead in order for His body to work properly. If you are part of the problem, and not part of the solution in your local body, or if you can't follow the leadership that He has placed in your body, then you must find somewhere that you can follow. Individually, we must each manifest the fruits of the Spirits in our local church, and if we are doing otherwise, we are hurting the body, not helping it–may it never be!

It's so important that we are in a place where there is unity, and we are each responsible to help build and bring the unity. Anything other than that is bringing the wrong fruit forward and is not of God. Why would we want to be in that kind of place? If we are the ones bringing bad fruit forward, why would we want to do that? We must continually check ourselves and our fruit. We need to think more about the health of the body than our own personal preferences. Sometimes we need to lay ourselves on the alter while He does His perfect work in each of us.

When there is a vindication of the Spirit, the gifts of the Spirit are evident.

1 Corinthians 12:4-7 says:

> Now there are varieties of gifts, but the same Spirit. And there are varieties of ministries, and the same Lord. There are varieties of effects, but the same God who works all things in all persons. But to each one is given a manifestation of the Spirit for the common good.

Gifts, ministries and effects include, but are not limited to: wisdom, knowledge, faith, healing, miracles, prophesy, distinguishing of spirits, tongues, interpretation of tongues, giving, teaching, exhortation, mercy, administration and helps. Apostle, Prophet, Evangelist, Teacher, and Pastor–these are manifestations that we should see in the church. Some are given by Christ, and some are given by the Spirit, but they are all manifestations that we should see in the church. When you study this, never ever, ever miss the end of verse 7–the manifestation of the Spirit is for the COMMON good. It is never meant for us personally.

It's meant for the common good; our giftings are always meant for others, not for ourselves–not to make a name, not to get a position, not to have notoriety. Our gifts will be most used, and actually increase, when we desire that other people benefit from them! That is when God opens them up and lets them flow.

When the Holy Spirit is vindicated, we begin to understand the deep things of God.

1 Corinthians 2:10-13 says:

> For to us, God revealed them through the Spirit; for the Spirit searches all things, even the depths of God. For who among men knows the thoughts of a man except the spirit of the man which is in him? Even so the thoughts of God no one knows except the Spirit of God. Now we receive not a spirit of this world, but the Spirit who is from God, so that we may know the things freely given to us by God, which things we also speak, not in words taught by human wisdom, but in those taught by the spirit, combining spiritual thoughts with spiritual words.

The Holy Spirit will give you revelation of God. The Spirit searches the deep things of God so that we can know what has been freely given to us. Who would we be if we received from the Holy Spirit the deep things of God that He already has for us? The Holy Spirit will give us revelation of God, but many believers have not experienced this yet, and it's part of the normal believer's walk! There is no greater personal desire that I have than to increase in my comprehension and experience of God's heart. When I am able to better grasp, understand, know and experience His character–when I understand His love–when I know His heart for me, it moves me in entirely new and fresh ways. It's a never-ending direction and process. I don't expect to ever fully get there this side of eternity, but I will continue to pursue Him.

Christianity has to become more than just being good, moral people while we wait for Jesus to return. There's a Kingdom to advance that we've been given responsibility over. Christianity is meant to be a powerful tool of salvation, for healing, for Kingdom building, territory taking, devil crushing, dominance over the enemy that results in joy, worship, and praise of a loving and victorious God! That's who we're supposed to be!

I want you to think about some of the past revivals you have heard of or been a part of. There are many we could mention, but a few more recent come to mind: Azusa Street, The Toronto Blessing, The Brownsville Revival, and The Lakeland Revival. In all of these, they were strong at one time and manifested His Glory. But what is also true is that they ended–there was a time or season that they lasted. Maybe the enemy got in. Things got squelched–maybe by man–but I believe revival is actually sustainable!

I believe revival is sustainable when we put the Word of God and the Spirit of God together. I believe it will be sustainable when these things become normal for us, when we make it normal for us to follow the instructions of Jesus, to be taught and guided by the Spirit and when we make it normal to be led by the Spirit. When the Holy Spirit is present and moving, it's exciting! When we experience moves of the Spirit in our corporate prayer, the Holy Spirit steps in and there is unity. There is excitement in our prayer. People have words, and there may be solemn times, or times of just laughing and joy, and talking and amen-ing each other as things begin to flow and naturally flows right into a worship set and everybody in the room can tell the Spirit's moving. It's like, WOW, this is unity! And that is just when we come together to pray! This is what we want and desire!

But I also want to mention a few things I believe the enemy tries to do. I believe when we see the schemes and plans of the enemy, we are aware in advance, we avoid them, and in the Spirit, we fight against them. There are things the enemy tries to do when there is a vindication of the Spirit in the church. When we decide we are going to follow Him and be guided by Him–to be taught by Him and work in the gifts, and let the fruits of the Spirit flow–here is the one thing that's sure to happen.

The enemy will use religion!

I talk about this a lot because it is a constant with a move of the Spirit. What is at the core is; religion needs rules so that it can condemn people in the body and keep them in a box. Rules enable religion to bring about a condemnation. For instance, "you cannot speak in tongues without interpretation." Rules keep things in a box and enable condemnation. Religion also brings routine for our comfort's sake, so that we become complacent with routine. Religion will create a business model out of the church instead of a family model that operates in unity and love. We need to recognize that the enemy will use religion to stop a move of the Holy Spirit. Man's rules and religion may keep him safe and secure, but the Holy Spirit moves freely outside of this box and religion.

The second thing the enemy does to stop a move of the Spirit is, he brings in division. He causes division between leaders. Why? If he can get the leader to stop progress or quit moving forward, whether by weariness, busyness, confusion, critique or any number of things, the whole mission stops. So there will be an attempt to bring division among the leaders. There will be division over doctrine. And this is important to know about division: division about doctrine is to create self-righteousness. This is how it may sound in the body, and I'm sure you've heard it: "I know what the Bible says... you're interpreting it wrong... I am right... You need to follow what I'm saying because I understand it and you don't." Self-righteous division will bring about pettiness to create distraction. It causes a zillion little problems so that we don't have time to deal with the big issue because we're fighting all the petty things. If the church can recognize and see the division, if they can recognize that the enemy has brought people in to try to destroy what Jesus and the Holy Spirit are about to do, that the enemy is going to attempt to come in and bust it up, then we can intercede and be proactive to stop it.

For instance, let me use a husband and wife as an example. When a husband and a wife can understand that God is about to do something with them, they will begin to experience fights between them. When they recognize the enemy, they will stop fighting each other because they recognize the enemy has brought a division in to cause the fight so they will be distracted from where God wants to take them. It's as simple as that, and it's the same way in the church. If we could see the division, the attempt of religion and self-righteousness, then we would say, "No way Jose, not on my dime, no way, no how, not in my house." We would say to each other, "I see you brother, and I'll sit down with you and let you know what I see the enemy doing right now in your life." We would say, "You're being used by the enemy, don't let it happen." When we see the enemy causing division, we can become instruments of unity in the church!

Another tool of the enemy is ridicule. This is vulnerable, but I've suffered a tremendous amount of ridicule in the last six years due to my stance on the Holy Spirit. I expect this ridicule to continue until those ridiculers get instantly healed of a disease! We will get ridiculed until the Pharisees among us start speaking in tongues! We will get ridiculed until the prophecies we speak come to pass! We will get ridiculed until the demon gets cast out of the tormented ridiculer! We will get ridiculed until the lost ridiculer gets saved! We will get ridiculed until a joy and a unity breaks out among us! We will get ridiculed until the people see a church led by the Spirit doing all the things that the Bible says believers can do! I want to be that church. That is the only church I want to be!

When we allow the Holy Spirit to come in, He changes the atmosphere and He brings about awe and wonder, excitement, anticipation, energy, enthusiasm and a love that maybe we haven't experienced yet. But when it comes about, we know it. We recognize; 'Here He comes!' Why? Because He's been invited, because we're open, because we're welcoming, and because we want to be guided, we want to be taught, and we want to be led by the Spirit. We must recognize that we have a divine opportunity in our territories. We have a divine opportunity right now in our territories to demonstrate what it means to be in the Kingdom of God, for the Holy Spirit to move, to heal, to deliver and to save. We have a divine opportunity right now, and we need to go for it!

I am going for it!

We are going for it!

We must go for it with the Word and with the Spirit. We've got to let go of that heart that has had so much religion, so much training, so much fear, so much accusation and condemnation. We've got to be fully open to the Holy Spirit. He can step in and say, "It's okay, I'll walk you through this, you don't understand it today, but I will guide you into the truth!" We can trust the Holy Spirit because He is our guide into all truth.

HOLY SPIRIT SIMPLIFICATION

We must know who the Holy Spirit is and His role and purpose in our lives. Who is the Holy Spirit, and when do we receive Him? If He is so important, why didn't we learn about Him before? How is the Holy Spirit connected to the gifts? To start, we're going to look in Genesis chapter one.

Genesis 1:2 says:

> The earth was formless and void, and darkness was over the surface of the deep, and the Spirit of God was moving over the surface of the waters.

This is what we know so far; from the very beginning of creation, the Holy Spirit has been in the picture. He is a prominent part of the Trinity: God the Father, Jesus the Son, and the Holy Spirit. Now we begin to look at how the Holy Spirit lives and moves and breathes in the lives of people. If we go to Genesis two, something happens that I believe we often overlook.

Genesis 2:7 says this:

> Then the Lord God formed man of dust from the ground, and breathed into his nostrils the breath of life; and man became a living being.

Different translations may say soul or being. This is part of the very first picture we get of the triad composition of man, but what exactly does this mean? It means that man is a body formed from the dust of the ground; that man has a spirit breathed into him by God; and that man has become a living soul. So, we have a soul, a body, and a spirit. First Thessalonians 5:23 reiterates this. We don't want to overlook what happened in the creation of man, but if we look at the Hebrew word here for breath, it is neshama. Neshama by definition in the Hebrew means, the spirit of God imparting life. If we believe that God formed man out of the dust of the ground and breathed oxygen into him, then we've missed it; that is not what happened. He didn't bring a body to life by blowing oxygen into his lungs to get them working. What He *did* was, He breathed *His very Spirit* into man in order to give him life. We're talking about *LIFE*, not just breath. We're not talking about just breathing and existing, we're talking about God using His very Spirit to give us life, the Spirit of life, the breath of life, the very substance of life, breathed from God's Spirit into man. That Spirit is key as we move forward because God tells Adam and Eve, if you eat from that tree, you will die, yet we know they didn't drop dead, we know their bodies didn't fall to the ground because they ate from it, we know that their soul continued because they continued to think and learn and have emotions. Adam and Eve had to be removed from the garden, yet they had children, built homes, raised families, and lived in a territory. Physically, mentally and in their soul, their lives went on, so what was missing? What was missing was the breath, the breath of life in their spirit. The spirit of man *became trapped and dead in sin*. Scripture even says in Ephesians that we are *dead in our trespasses and sin*, dead in the *spirit* of man, *not* in the body or the soul.

As we go through the Old Testament from that point forward, we don't see the Spirit living in and moving in man. What we do see is God releasing the Spirit at certain times for certain things. If we look in Exodus 31, God wants to build a tabernacle to dwell among man using a man named Bezalel. He wants some things made, like an Ark of the Covenant, candle stands and the table of showbread, and He gives the skills to build these things to Bezalel.

Now watch how He does that in Exodus 31:2-3:

> See, I have called by name Bezalel, the son of Uri, the son of Hur, of the tribe of Judah. I have filled him with the Spirit of God in wisdom, in understanding, in knowledge, and in all kinds of craftsmanship, to make artistic designs for work in gold, in silver, and in

> bronze, and in the cutting of stones for settings, and in the carving of wood, that he may work in all kinds of craftsmanship.

So God fills him with the Spirit in order for him to do these things. We see it again in Numbers 11 with Moses and his 70 leaders. Moses is a bit overwhelmed when God tells him you need some leaders that have the same qualities you have.

Let's look in Numbers 11:24-25:

> So Moses went out and told the people the words of the Lord. Also, he gathered 70 men of the elders of the people, and stationed them around the tent. Then the Lord came down in a cloud and spoke to him; and He took of the Spirit who was upon him and placed Him upon the 70 elders. And when the Spirit rested upon them, they prophesied. But they did not do it again.

What we see happening here is that, in order for the 70 to serve as leaders, they had to have the Holy Spirit upon them as the Holy Spirit was on Moses.

In Numbers, we see a man named Balaam. Numbers 24:2 says:

> And Balaam lifted up his eyes and he saw Israel camping tribe by tribe and the Spirit of God came upon him.

In Judges 14:6, we see a man named Samson dealing with a lion:

> The Spirit of the Lord came upon him mightily, so that he tore him as one tears a young goat though he had nothing in his hand; but he did not tell his father and mother what he'd done.

On and on we see God stepping in and pouring His Spirit out on individuals and saying, "Here, I need you to do this, I have a job for you, I have a purpose, I'm going to give you the Spirit to do these things." Then as we read on in scripture through the prophets, we begin to see a consistent prophecy, the telling of something that's coming, a prophesy that concerns the Spirit and an individual.

In Isaiah 42:1, God is speaking, and He says:

> Behold, My servant, whom I uphold; My chosen one *in whom* My soul delights. I have put my Spirit upon him; He will bring forth justice to the nations.

So the people are encouraged that a Messiah is coming. God is going to put His Spirit on the Messiah who is going to bring peace to the nations. But then there's another prophecy in Joel that seems to expand this idea of the Spirit. In Joel two it says there was a great invasion going on and there was a rescue by the Lord and it comes to this conclusion in verses 28-29:

> It will come about after this that I will pour out my Spirit on all mankind; and your sons and your daughters will prophesy, Your old men will dream dreams, Your young men will see visions. Even on the male and female servants I will pour out My Spirit in those days.

God says, I will pour out my Spirit in those days, and that's really critical! It's also critical that He said, even on the servants. Why? Because back when He was committing to a covenant relationship with Abraham, He said, I want you to circumcise every one and that will be a sign of their covenant relationship with me. But then if a purchased servant is in your household, I want you to circumcise him too. He will be under the same covenant. The servant in his household would have been a Gentile; in this case, the prophecy is saying that even to the Gentiles, even those outside of my people, the servants that are bought, will be under the same covenant. That prophetic word indicates that anyone "bought with a price" is under the covenant with God. In other words, every redeemed believer is bought with a price, Jesus. So this Messiah comes, He is Jesus, and they're expecting Him to reign over all the earth and for peace to come to all nations because Jesus has arrived.

But something different happens, something very different for them. Something that really confused them, Jesus gets crucified. This Messiah that they've been waiting for, who will rule and reign and bring peace to all the nations, is put to death. These guys have been following Him for three years, and they are very confused. But because they've supported Him as the coming Messiah, the one that would take over, the Jewish nation is now angry with them because they supported a false Messiah, so they're afraid. They actually hide in fear after the crucifixion of Jesus. They go to a room and huddle together because they don't know what to do. We see in Acts 2 that they did not understand the scripture that Jesus must be raised from the dead, so they hid together in fear.

But in John Chapter 20, we hear a story that most of us have probably not thought of before; we are going to see two things put together, and they will make sense. In John Chapter 20 it's the first day of the week, the day of the resurrection. Mary has now gone to the tomb and it is empty, so she brings back a few of the disciples, they see the same, and they don't know what to do. So they go back and hide out in this room, and in John 20:19 something happens in the room, and it looks like this:

> So when it was evening on that day, the first day of the week,

So what day are we talking about? We need to go back to verse one which shows us that it is the first day of the week when they find the tomb empty, and we are still in the same day. Mary goes back and tells the disciples, the disciples also run and find the tomb empty, then they go back to this room, and it says "on that day," which is going to be important. On that day, the first day of the week, when it was evening on that same day, we see in scripture:

> …and when the doors were shut, where the disciples were for fear of the Jews, Jesus came and stood in their midst and he said to them, "Peace be with you."

And we would have thought the room would have erupted, wow, Jesus, this is amazing! But they didn't. Jesus said, "Peace be with you" and I'm telling you, they just looked at Him. How do I know that? Look at this next verse 20:

> And when He had said this, He showed them both of His hands and His side.

What is he doing? He is revealing that it is actually Him, Jesus, resurrected. He is proving, "I was the one who was crucified, I am standing in front of you." Then it clicks, and that's when they understand. How do we know that? Look at the next line, after this occurrence of Him showing the scars,

> The disciples then rejoiced when they saw the Lord.

So we can see that He comes in and says, "Peace be with you." And they say, "Who are you?" And He, Jesus, says guys, it's me, look at my scars. Then they rejoiced and said, this is the risen savior! This guy was crucified, and now He's alive! This is so important to us, why? Because that's the gospel presentation, that He died for our sins, that He was crucified to take on our condemnation, that He was resurrected for our justification, and that He was raised to show us that He can give us eternal life. So what happens next? It's critical to remember that it's still the first day of the week, the same day He's raised from the dead. So Jesus said to them in verse 21 and 22:

> "Peace be with you; as the Father has sent Me, I also send you." And when He had said this, He breathed on them and said to them, "Receive the Holy Spirit."

I don't know if you saw what just happened. Do you remember back at creation, that God made man out of the dust of the ground and He breathed His Spirit into him to give him life? So Jesus tells them what He has just done for them; He says, *now you believe* in the *crucifixion* and the *resurrection*, so *I'm going to breathe the Spirit of God back into you to give you life now and for eternity*! It's a re-creation. It's a restoration of the garden. Now the Spirit can dwell *IN* man, now the Spirit can walk *with* man, this is where the Holy Spirit comes back to dwell in and with man, and *this is HUGE*! *Jesus has breathed the Holy Spirit back into man!* This is awesome because they now *fully* understand the gospel. But this is not what is taught doctrinally or in theology. Seminary classes usually don't teach that one be indwelled by the Holy Spirit in this way. Sealed, yes, indwelled, no.

We cannot be saved until we have heard and understood the gospel message, and the gospel message is that we are sinful, that we are separated from God in our sin, and that God sent Christ as a man who never sinned. Why is this so important? It's important because with Christ's death, burial and resurrection, our relationship with God for eternal life is fully restored! He who knew no sin, Jesus, became sin on our behalf 'so that' we might take *His* standing of righteousness before the Father. What does this mean? It means that, even though we have sinned, when we believe that Christ came for us personally, died for our sin, and was resurrected to show us that there is life after this one and that He will give us eternal life when we personally receive Him, when we believe this, we are righteous before God. Because Christ took our condemnation from us at the cross, we stand righteous before God!

So what happened in the room where the disciples were hiding? The Apostles could not actually be saved until they 'believed' in the death and the resurrection according to Romans 10:9 and 10, and other scriptures:

> That if you confess with your mouth Jesus as Lord, and believe in your heart that God raised Him from the dead, you will be saved; for with the heart a person believes, resulting in righteousness, and with the mouth he confesses, resulting in salvation.

This is the moment where they recognize this person is the resurrected Christ, and now they can have the Holy Spirit imparted to them, now they can be sealed for the day of redemption!

So I'm going to take you to Ephesians chapter 1. God, in the form of Jesus, has returned that breath of life, returned that Spirit of God, to man. And in Ephesians 1 this is what it says in verse 13:

> In Him, you also, after listening to the message of truth, the gospel of your salvation–having also believed, you were sealed in Him with the Holy Spirit of promise, who is given as a pledge of our inheritance, with a view to the redemption of God's own possession, to the praise of His glory.

What does this mean? It means that when we hear the gospel, when we understand that His death, burial, and resurrection was for us, and that when we believe, we are sealed with the Holy Spirit for the day of redemption. This is a pledge of our inheritance, the pledge that the Holy Spirit comes and seals us. This is the pledge of our eternal life, of our inheritance. This is what happens when we believe: we are sealed with the Spirit and given the Spirit as a pledge of our inheritance; we now have the Holy Spirit. That breath of God has been breathed back into us. It's that simple; when we believe, we are sealed with the Spirit and given the Spirit as a pledge of our inheritance.

We have now received the Holy Spirit, but is that it? No, it's not, because we have to understand the complete story, which includes another man who came along and talked about something different. At first, the disciples didn't understand it, but this man's name was John the Baptist. He's described as a rough and rugged man who wore wild clothes made of camel's hair and ate locusts and honey, but he also had a story to tell. In Luke 3:16, John the Baptist says:

> John answered and said to them all, "As for me, I baptize you with water.

If you don't know the story, it was foretold that John the Baptist would come before the Christ. He was to preach repentance, meaning they needed to change their minds, because the Messiah was coming. They needed to turn from evil. They needed to be washed with water, so they were baptized. Verse sixteen continues:

> "As for me, I baptize you with water; but One is coming who is mightier than I, and I am not fit to untie

> the thong of His sandals; He will baptize you with the Holy Spirit."

This is what John said in summary, there is Jesus, and when He comes, He's going to baptize you with the Holy Spirit.

Now we've got to go back to the room where the disciples were hiding. To review, Jesus has been resurrected from the dead and has met with His disciples. He showed them who He was and breathed on them and said, "receive the Holy Spirit," so now they have the Holy Spirit. But remember the calendar day from John 20? It was the first day of the week, the first day of the resurrection, so now we fast forward to Acts chapter one. Let's watch as Luke, the author of Acts, explains to Theophilus all things about Jesus. In Acts 1:1-3 Luke says:

> The first account I composed, Theophilus, about all that Jesus began to do and teach *(the first account was the book of Luke),* until the day when He was taken up to heaven, after He had by the Holy Spirit given orders to the apostles whom He had chosen. To these He also presented Himself alive after his suffering.

Jesus shows up in the room and says, "guys, it's me, it's Jesus." He has presented himself as alive from the dead.

> By many convincing proofs, appearing to them over a period of 40 days and speaking concerning the Kingdom of God.

So what's the story? Christ has been crucified, resurrected, and has shown Himself to the apostles. He has breathed on them and said, "now you've received the Holy Spirit, and for the next 40 days, I'm going to teach you about the Kingdom of God. I'm going to help you understand this Kingdom." So after appearing to them over 40 days and speaking of the things concerning the Kingdom of God, we see in verses 4 and 5:

> Gathering them together, He commanded them not to leave Jerusalem, but to wait for what the Father had promised, "Which," He said, "you heard from Me for John the Baptist baptized with water but you will be baptized with the Holy Spirit not many days from now."

So the baptism in the Spirit was a separate event from Jesus breathing on them to receive the Holy Spirit as we saw in John 20. Jesus has given them the Holy Spirit and says, now wait, because not many days from now you're going to be baptized in the Spirit. It is 40 days after he has given them the Holy Spirit, and now he is saying wait because in not many days I will baptize you in the Holy Spirit. Maybe you are wondering, is it possible that this meeting in Acts is the same meeting as the one on the first day? It doesn't really matter which line of thinking you want to take, either He gathered them, and this conversation is still on that first day or we're talking about 40 days later, which is what I personally believe. Either way, I don't know how one can get more scripturally clear that there is a separate baptism in the Spirit not many days from now, and it is different than the first time they were given the Spirit!

We receive the Holy Spirit when we receive Christ, when He 'breathed on them', but then He says, "you will be baptized in the Holy Spirit not many days from now." These are separate events, and they are separate in scripture. Christ is telling the very Apostles that were following him, "I gave you the Holy Spirit, but not many days from now, whether it's 10 or whether it's 50, you're going to be baptized in the Spirit with fire." Woo hoo, come on, lets stop debating a separate baptism in the Holy Spirit, the scripture is very clear on this!

So what did that baptism look like? When we go to Acts chapter 2, when the day of Pentecost had come, which was "not many days from now," the day of Pentecost was here, and in verses 1-4:

> When the day of Pentecost had come, they were all together in one place. And suddenly there came from heaven a noise like a violent rushing wind, and it filled

> the whole house where they were sitting. And there appeared to them tongues as of fire distributing themselves, and they rested on each one of them. And they were all filled with the Holy Spirit and began to speak with other tongues, as the Spirit was giving them utterance.

But wait, didn't they already have the Holy Spirit, which we learned in John 20? Didn't Jesus breathe on them and say, "receive the Holy Spirit?" But now the Holy Spirit is "coming upon them" and they're being *"filled"* with the Spirit. When 'this' occurrence of the Spirit coming upon them happens, something very unique occurs with it. The disciples began to speak with other tongues as the Spirit was giving them utterance. If you're unsure about tongues, let's sit with this for a moment and recognize that something miraculous is happening. And to clarify, something miraculous did not begin to happen when Jesus met with them the day of His resurrection, when He 'breathed on them' and said, "receive the Holy Spirit". It never says in John 20 that they started speaking in tongues at that time. What He did say was, "*wait*, and not many days from now, the Holy Spirit will come upon you," and "but you will be baptized with the Holy Spirit not many days from now." *This* is the baptism in the Spirit that He was talking about, which is a different event from the Holy Spirit that Jesus imparted when He breathed on them in John 20.

The first is an impartation of the Holy Spirit, and the second is a baptism or immersion of the Holy Spirit. Do you see that?

So let's summarize so far. Jesus shares with the disciples in John 20 what has just happened, and then He breathes on them. I believe in that moment, the breath of life comes and they are sealed with the Holy Spirit as a pledge, or confirmation, of their (our) eternal life and inheritance. Then, not many days from now, they would be baptized in the Spirit where the Spirit comes upon them with power. So the next question would be, can we prove this multi-step sequence in scripture? Can we see where this happened in the Bible?

Let's look at Acts 19:1-6:

> It happened that while Apollos was at Corinth, Paul passed through the upper country and came to Ephesus, and found some disciples. He said to them, "Did you receive the Holy Spirit when you believed?"

So in the conversation, belief is already there, "when you believed." They are definitely believers, they are saved. So Paul is asking, did the Holy Spirit come upon you when you believed?

And they said to him, *like a lot of denominational teaching,*

> "*No, we have not even heard whether there is a Holy Spirit.*"
>
> And he said, "Into what then were you baptized?" And they said, "Into John's baptism." Paul said, "John baptized with the baptism of repentance, telling people to believe in Him who was coming after him, that is, in Jesus." When they heard this, they were baptized in the name of the Lord Jesus.

So now they are water baptized in the name of Jesus. Then Paul lays hands on them.

> And when Paul laid his hands upon them, the Holy Spirit came upon them, and they began speaking with tongues and prophesying.

Are you seeing it? They believed, therefore they are sealed, indwelled by the Spirit, receiving the pledge of their inheritance, baptized in water, and now baptized in the Spirit.

So what are we learning fundamentally about the Holy Spirit? From the very beginning, God breathed the breath of life, His very Spirit, into man. Man then rejects Him and that spirit part of the relationship died. Man, dead in his trespasses and sins, with his soul and his body, continued looking for restoration to God. God would on occasion bring the Holy Spirit to a person in order for them to accomplish something that God needed them to accomplish. But He said, one day I'll send My son, and when He comes and you believe in what He has done, you will be sealed with the Holy Spirit. Your spirit will be regenerated and you will have that indwelling of the Holy Spirit as a pledge to your inheritance. Then, maybe not many days from now, you'll be baptized in the Spirit. It's not complicated. The Spirit comes, the Spirit indwells, the Spirit seals. Then you can have the baptism of the Holy Spirit.

Why would one want to be baptized in the Spirit? I'll tell you why for me, because for 30 years I was a believer who was not baptized in the Spirit. Let me tell you what the life of a believer, not baptized in the Spirit, is like. I did not understand why all these things in the Bible happened for them, but not for me. I did not understand a word of knowledge or a word of wisdom. I did not understand tongues or how to prophesy. What was prophecy? Did they just encourage people, or was there a gift of prophecy where you actually get a word from God? I did not get to work in those things. I believed, and was in love with Jesus, in love with the Word of God, but because of my upbringing, I was fully rejecting a baptism in the Spirit.

I was told we received the Holy Spirit when we received salvation, yet we didn't talk about Him much, certainly not like we talked about Jesus. That was everything I learned 'until,' until I read this line in scripture where Jesus, who had already given them the Spirit, said "wait here, and not many days from now," as John told you, "I'm going to baptize you in the Spirit." That became a doctrinal problem for me because *it said they already had the Spirit* and *then they got baptized in the Spirit.* Suddenly I had to listen to some of these people I'd been rejecting for a long time who had been saying a believer can be baptized in the Spirit. What does that baptism of the Spirit bring? It brings the miraculous! That's the only way I can describe it, it brings tongues, prophecy, words of wisdom, words of knowledge, and healing!

Did you know that scripture actually says there is a gift of miracles? What if we have the gift of miracles, and it just hasn't been released yet? What would our life look like? Maybe good, but not great, because we might be missing out on all of these important things we're supposed to release for people. All of a sudden we begin working in new things we didn't understand before. We see the reality of how walking in the power of the Spirit edifies the believer!

It might be helpful for me to share some of my first experiences after being baptized in the Spirit. I had never prophesied, not more than just encouraging someone and building them up, but I wasn't working in the gift of prophecy. Quickly I began working in the gift of prophecy, and the Spirit began to give me words for people. "Say this to this person," or I would get a picture in my mind of something I was supposed to tell them. I would take the risk and tell the person about the picture.

One Wednesday evening I was at the front of our auditorium available to pray with people, and a young lady walked up to me and I began to pray. The Spirit gave me a vision that I knew I was supposed to tell her. But to be honest, I really didn't want to tell her because the vision seemed way out of place and bizarre; but I was new to the baptism in the Spirit and wanted to walk by faith, so I began to tell her what I saw. I told her that I saw a pizza that was broken into pieces on a cooking sheet, then I saw two hands pushing it back together. After the pieces were back in place, I saw the hands putting fresh cheese on top of the pizza so that when it cooked it would be a whole pizza again. Now honestly, I felt really stupid saying these things to her. I could not imagine why the Spirit would have a pastor pray about pizza over someone. Then I got a little more from the Spirit. I told her I believed the Spirit was saying her life was fragmented and that He would be putting it back together. She smiled and walked away. I felt dumb.

But the following Sunday this same lady was in a class where she had the opportunity to give a testimony. When invited to the front to share, she said that she wanted to testify about something that had happened earlier in the week. She said it happened the previous Wednesday. She had to work late but still wanted to come to church, so she went home to find the quickest thing she could eat for dinner and still make it to church. The quickest thing she could make was a frozen pizza. But when she opened the package it was all broken into pieces. She put the pieces on a cooking sheet, pushing them back together and adding some fresh cheese to the top to hold it together.

Then she said, when I got to church the Pastor prayed for me and told me all about the pizza incident I had just had at home. So I guess the Lord is telling me my life is a bit fragmented, but He will put me back together. Now I realized why I had said that and was glad I had listened to the Lord.

On a Sunday morning a man came up to me with a medical report. He had tumors on both of his kidneys and was scheduled for an operation. He showed me on the report the exact size and location of the tumors on each kidney. He was schedule for an operation that week to remove the tumors. He asked me to pray for him, so I did. The following Sunday he came to church with a big smile on his face. He said that when he went to the hospital for the surgery and the doctors decided to take one more x-ray before the surgery just in case the tumors had grown. After the x-rays were taken, the doctor came in and cancelled his surgery because the tumors were gone.

On another Sunday, I had been giving some words. As I was walking across the congregation, there sat Mark; and this is what the Spirit said, "Tell him some money's about to come his way." Now as a pastor, I'm not a prosperity gospel guy. It's not about us getting rich, so I thought to the Holy Spirit, you want me to prophesize money so that everybody can look at me and say, "Yep, just another charismatic pastor who thinks it's all about money." So this is what I did. I was walking across the auditorium because there was another lady I had a word for. So quickly, I looked at Mark and said, "some money's coming your way," and I just went on because although I'd been walking in prophecy, there were times when I thought, Holy Spirit, is that you or me? I chickened out on giving the full word, and said it quickly in passing. Then Mark came back to me two weeks later and said, "I got the biggest raise I've ever gotten in one chunk in my entire life!"

It would be easy to think, "You lucked out on that one, Todd." It's a coincidence until you've seen it happen 50 times, and you realize God has endued you with the power to be able to speak into other people's lives through the gift of prophecy. He can endue you with power through the gift of tongues. He endues us with power through our faith. We can have the faith to move in things that *others aren't willing to move in*. We can *give in ways that other people are not willing to give*, we can work in the miraculous! There are gifts of healing, and what if those things are waiting to be released to us in the baptism of the Spirit? What if we laid hands on people and they got healed, would that not change our Christian walk? We go from, I'm trying to be good God so I can get to heaven, to bring me somebody so I can watch them get healed!

Simplification is when we believe the gospel, when we believe that Christ died to pay for our sins, when we believe that he gave us His righteousness, when we believe that He was raised from the dead to give us eternal life. We inherit salvation and are sealed by the Holy Spirit, *then the Holy Spirit can come upon us in the baptism in the Spirit to work in power*!

Corinthians 6 says this:

> Or do you not know that your body is a temple of the Holy Spirit who is in you, whom you have from God, and that you're not on your own? For you have been bought with a price: therefore glorify God in your body.

1 John 4:15:

> Whoever confesses that Jesus is the Son of God, God abides in him and he in God.

Ephesians 4:30:

> Do not grieve the Holy Spirit of God, by whom you were sealed for the day of redemption.

2 Corinthians 1:21:

> Now He who establishes us with you in Christ and anointed us is God, who also sealed us and gave us the Spirit in our hearts as a pledge.

I believe there are three kinds of people reading this book. The first hasn't stepped out to trust Christ yet for their salvation. It's the biggest decision you will ever make because it's the only one that changes your eternity. It's the opportunity for Christ to take care of all of your transgressions before God. He is willing to take them to the cross and die with them in your name and give you His righteous standing before God; all of your condemnation is taken care of in Christ when you put your trust in him for your salvation.

Then there's a second group reading this book. You've been walking not only as a believer, but you've also been baptized in the Spirit. But my guess is, you're frustrated. You're frustrated that the Kingdom of God does not seem to be more powerful in you and in your territory. When we have believers who are baptized in the Spirit but they are not walking it out, not healing the sick, not raising the dead, not cleansing the leper, they are frustrated. They are frustrated because they know there's more, and they're wondering why these things are not happening for them when they know they can. How do we help that group move forward?

I believe we need to step out and take risks. If we're not in a church or with a body of believers where this is encouraged, we might need to find a place where we can grow in this way. At least for a while, we need to absorb more, learn more, grow more; sometimes we need to be in a place where we can practice or learn from watching others. Either way, we need to stop and pray for the sick and infirmed for healing, listening to the Holy Spirit to hear what words we might have for people. As believers, it's who we are supposed to be, it's who we are in the Kingdom of God. That's how we will change a territory. That's how the name of God, the name of Jesus, and the Kingdom of God, will be elevated in a territory, because a group of believers is going to stand up and say, "Enough silencing the Holy Spirit! Enough letting the sick remain sick! Enough letting those in bondage remain in bondage! Enough! Let's operate in the power of the Spirit, it's time to set the captives free."

Then there's a third group, and I would really like to focus on this group. This is a group like I was for 30 years, believing the things of Christ, wanting to be faithful and true, but man, just lacking power.

It was always a struggle. Don't misunderstand me, I would see God come through for me and work powerfully on my behalf and answer my prayers, and yet I had no authority to do anything. The only thing I had authority to do was to ask God to help me. But in 2013, I was in the middle of a church service and I got baptized in the Spirit!

As a pastor, I dropped to the floor weeping and sobbing so hard I couldn't breathe and the Spirit said to me, "You've been talking about me for years, now, it's time for you to get to know me." All of a sudden a language that I'd never spoken before came. All of a sudden I could walk up to someone and God would say, "Tell him to let it go. Just tell him to let it go," and for no reason at all, that person would break down crying. And all I said was "let it go" and he did! I was hearing from the Spirit!

God wants to work miraculously through you and with power to demonstrate His love. Paul, when he came to Corinth to teach, said, I didn't come to convince you with words. I came to convince you with the power of the Holy Spirit.

My prayer for you is this:

Father God, I release my belief, my faith, and my courage. I know God that the things you have set up for me are true. I know the Holy Spirit is waiting to baptize me. So in the name of Jesus, I just bring forth that courage to believe. For those who have wondered or waited, for those who are ready, I ask you to baptize them in the Holy Spirit now! Right now I ask you to release the Holy Spirit into their life with miracles, signs and wonders, with gifting, and with ministries. Baptize them with all of the supernatural gifts of the Spirit. Bring it to them now, God. In Jesus name!

HOLY SPIRIT INTOXICATION

Let's talk about Holy Spirit intoxication. I realize this title may give some grief, but bear with me because it's going make sense when you read the scripture. We're going to start with Ephesians 5:15-21:

> Therefore be careful how you walk, not as unwise men, but as wise, making the most of your time, because the days are evil. So then do not be foolish, but understand what the will of the Lord is. And do not get drunk with wine, for that is dissipation, but be filled with the Spirit, speaking to one another in psalms, and hymns, and spiritual songs, singing and making melody with your heart to the Lord; always giving thanks for all things in the name of our Lord Jesus Christ to God, even the father; and be subject to one another in the fear of Christ.

Make the most of your time. It says a wise person would make the most of their time. And I want to use this scripture to explain what is making the most of your time. Follow me on this; it says your time spent is weighed against the evil days. Your time is measured against the evil of this day. So, to make the most of your time, you will be in opposition to the evil of the day. Again, make the most of your time because the days are evil. Do not be foolish, but understand the will of the Lord. So instead of being unwise and foolish, in order for us to be wise, we must understand the will of the Lord. You notice it said, do not be foolish, but understand what the will of the Lord is.

So the contrast is: foolishness in the days of evil, to wisdom with the will of the Lord. Does this make sense? So foolishness comes from submitting to the evil in our days, and wisdom comes from submitting to the will of the Lord in our time. Got it? Let's repeat this, foolishness comes from submitting to the evil in our days, and wisdom comes from submitting to the will of the Lord in our time. So understanding that our life is the time to serve the Lord's will, and abstaining from evil is making the most of our time.

Now Paul goes on from here to talk about getting drunk with wine, and I think it's important to cover that. I want to dig into this scripture because he contrasts getting drunk with wine with being filled with the Holy Spirit. He says, if we are filled with wine, it brings dissipation, and dissipation is a unique Greek word that means an abandoned life, a wasteful life. In other words, you have given up or you've decided to waste life if you choose to be filled with wine. But to be filled with the Holy Spirit, according to this scripture, brings songs, thankfulness and submission.

So you might ask, why does he compare being filled with the Spirit to being filled with wine or what we would call drunkenness? Why would we even want to put those two things in a category together? Wouldn't that cast a shadow on being filled with the Spirit if somehow you compared it to being filled with wine or drunkenness? I think the answer is in the book of Acts, chapter 2. We all know this story in Acts chapter 2; Jesus tells his disciples to wait in Jerusalem until the Holy Spirit has come upon them. They're in an upper room, the sound of a mighty rushing wind comes in, and tongues of fire are distributed on each of them. Then they each began to speak in other tongues as the Spirit gave them utterance. I think it's important to read through several scriptures, so we'll start in Acts 2:6. This is after the Spirit has come in this way, and it says:

> And when this sound occurred, the crowd came together, and were bewildered because each one of them was hearing them speak in his own language.

So the crowd is bewildered that these men who are Galileans, who should not know how to speak their language, are speaking their languages. And they're wondering how in the world the disciples can speak my language. Let's look down in verse 12, where it says:

> And they all continued in amazement and great perplexity, saying to one another. "What does this mean?" But others were mocking and saying, "They are full of sweet wine."

Now here's the context of where I want to go with this scripture. Why would it be that if you began speaking in my language and I know you don't know my language, that I would think you were drunk? Is it just the ability to speak in my language that somehow makes me think you're drunk? Quite honestly, if I spoke a different language and you begin to speak to me in my language, which I knew you didn't know, I wouldn't think you were drunk. I would just say, "That is totally cool! That's amazing that you can do that!" But in verse 11, it says:

> Cretins and Arabs–we hear them in our own tongues speaking of the mighty deeds of God.

Now this is interesting because I think a lot of people miss this when they study the day of Pentecost. When they began to speak in tongues, they did not begin to share the gospel. Although they were speaking in the language of the people who are in Jerusalem, the scripture never says they began to share the gospel. As a matter of fact, later Peter gathers everybody together and shares the Gospel, but it says what the rest of them were doing was speaking of the mighty deeds of God. And when they were speaking of the mighty deeds of God in someone else's language, the people thought they were drunk. It's still confusing to me. So now they're speaking to people in their language, which we know they didn't know, and they're talking about the mighty deeds of God. And for some reason that makes the people think they are drunk. It doesn't make sense! Peter confirms that everyone thought they were drunk, and in verse 15-17 Peter stands up and says:

> For these men are not drunk, as you suppose, for it is only the third hour of the day (which is nine o'clock in the morning); but this is what was spoken of through the Prophet Joel: 'And it shall be in the last days', God says, 'That I will pour forth of my Spirit on all

> mankind; And your sons and your daughters shall prophesy, And your young men shall see visions, And your old men shall dream dreams;'

So the Spirit was poured out on them, and they began speaking in other languages about the mighty deeds of God. But look, something about the way they were doing that made the people think they were drunk. Something about how they were expressing the mighty deeds of God at nine o'clock in the morning made the people think, you've got to be drunk because of how you're doing this. So then the question is, is there anywhere we can reference in scripture that would help us understand how they were doing it that would make everyone think they were drunk? Of course there is, or I wouldn't have brought it up. Let's go to Psalm 71:16-24

> I will come with the mighty deeds of the Lord God; I will make mention of Your righteousness, Yours alone, O God, You have taught me from my youth, And I still declare your wondrous deeds, and even when I am old and gray, O God, do not forsake me, until I declare your strength to this generation, Your power to all who are to come. For your righteousness, O God, reaches to the heavens, You who have done great things; O God, who is like you? You have shown me many troubles and distresses, will revive me again, and will bring me up again from the depths of the earth. May you increase my greatness and turn to comfort me. I will also praise you with a harp, even Your truth, O my God; To You I will sing praises with the lyre, Oh Holy One of Israel. My Lips will shout for joy when I sing praises to You; and my soul, which You have redeemed. My tongue also will utter Your righteousness all day long; For they are ashamed, for they are humiliated who seek my hurt.

What did you hear about how they were proclaiming the mighty deeds of God in this scripture? They were doing it with declarations, without stopping, with praises, singing and shouting. So let's go back to what happened on the day of Pentecost. When the Spirit came down, they began to speak in other languages, but they were praising and singing and shouting to God of His mighty deeds. And these people were hearing it in their own language in such a way that they thought, "You guys have to be drunk to be that happy at nine o'clock in the morning! You guys are shouting and singing and praising about your God, and it's so early that there must be some drinking involved in this." But being filled with the Spirit can bring about a joy and rejoicing and excitement that will make us sing and shout and yell out and declare our praises to God, and others will think we're drunk.

Let's go back to the original scripture in Ephesians; it says they were speaking to one another in psalms, hymns, spiritual songs, singing and making melody with their heart to the Lord. It says, when you are filled with the Spirit, you will speak to one another in psalms, and hymns, and spiritual songs, singing and making melody with your heart to the Lord. Let's look at the individual words without getting hung up on them. We know what hymns are, classic hymns like Amazing Grace and How Great Thou Art, and we know what psalms are, songs from the Psalms, such as, Bless the Lord Oh My Soul and Better is One Day in Your Courts. We have hymns, psalms, spiritual songs, and melodies that arise spontaneously during worship; they arise in the spirit, songs that originate in a moment of singing in the Spirit.

I don't want to overly focus on the definition of psalms, hymns, and spiritual songs because the next thing we'll do is decide we have to do each one of these, and in a certain balance or order to be doing things biblically. Then we'll end up making a rule out of how these should be done properly in a service, and that's not the focus, but that's not what he's talking about. What he's talking about is making the best of your time by being filled with the Spirit, and scripture says we will be speaking to one another in: *psalms and hymns and spiritual songs, singing and making a melody with a heart to the Lord, always giving thanks for all things in the name of our Lord Jesus Christ to God, even the Father, and be subject to one another in the fear of Christ.*

It's an interesting point. I don't know if you saw it, but it says that we're to be singing and making a melody with our hearts, not just singing a melody, but creating a melody with our hearts. We're not talking about our physical hearts, or just singing songs, it's about making a melody 'with' our hearts. When we examine this scripture regarding what it means for us, some questions arise as to how we do this, how do we make a melody with a heart to the Lord? How do we raise up praise to God that comes from our hearts? Is there a melody about the Lord that is within us?

Where does our voice of praise come from, our tongue, or from our hearts? Do we have a melody that needs to be released to the Lord? Can we be in a place that is a constant state of thanksgiving to God in and through the name of Jesus? And, can we be in unity with other believers in this? When I read these verses, I begin asking these questions because I think all of these things are possible when I'm *intoxicated* with Holy Spirit, and unfortunately, the world will think I'm drunk. I get that, but there's also a joy in a melody that rises up inside of me, and I'm more concerned with what 'He' thinks than what others think.

Another point we see in this scripture is that it says they were doing this speaking to one another. Isn't that interesting, because typically when you hear about a song or a psalm, it is to God. But it says in this scripture that they were doing this 'to' one another. Why would we be doing this 'to' one another? I believe this speaks to unity in the Spirit because if we go to Genesis 11, we see the story of the Tower of Babel, and at the Tower of Babel the Lord says in 11:6:

> The Lord said, "Behold they are one people, and they all have the same language. And this is what they began to do, and now nothing which they propose to do will be impossible for them. Come, let Us go down and there confuse their language so they will not understand one another's speech."

In other words, there is unity and strength in a common language. We know that the Old Testament is a physical representation of the spiritual concept under the New Covenant, so with this in mind, what does the Tower of Babel represent? We're talking about a unity in our language so that we can have strength, but it's not in our physical language. It's in the language of the Holy Spirit. In other words, there is a melody that is in our hearts that we want to release in the spiritual realm, and the melody in our hearts will come into harmony with others because there is unity in the Spirit. When we have a common language in the Spirit from the heart, we have *strength*! So, there's a language that we speak that's not with our mouth or words, it's with our heart. It's with our spirit. Strength is the outcome when the connection, the language and unity in the Spirit come together with others because we're coming in alignment using the language of God. Unity through a common language *from our hearts* in the Spirit! That's powerful!

This has been foundational for us to understand and receive the next point, which is to understand the comparison between getting drunk with wine and being filled with the Holy Spirit. When one is filled with wine, they are using drunkenness to think less about their problems. But, when we are filled with the Holy Spirit, we are using the Spirit to remind us of the resources that we have to deal with our problems! It's the total opposite, one is trying to numb our spirits not to deal with our problems, and the other is using the resource of the Holy Spirit to deal with our problems, and it works like this.

When we are drunk with wine, our minds are in the flesh, and we are weary and tired. But when we are drunk with the Spirit, we are actively aware that when we wait for the Lord, we renew our strength and mount up with wings like eagles. We run without getting tired, and we walk without being weary. (Isaiah 40:31)

When we are drunk with wine, we think we are weak; but when we are filled with the Spirit, we know that greater is He who is in me than He who is in the world. (1 John 4:4)

When we are drunk with wine, we've got a target on our backs. But when we are filled with the Spirit, there is no weapon formed against us that can prosper; and every tongue that accuses us in judgment, God will condemn. This is the heritage of the servants of the Lord, and our vindication is from the Lord. (Isaiah 54:17)

When we are filled with wine, we cry ourselves to sleep. But when we are filled with the Spirit, we know that weeping lasts for the night, but joy comes in the morning. (Psalm 30:5)

When we are drunk with wine, we have no help. But when we are filled with the Spirit, we know that He is able to do far more abundantly beyond all that we ask or think according to His power that works within us. (Ephesians 3:20)

Let's look at this scripture at a deeper level, Ephesians 3:20:

> Now to Him who is able to do far more abundantly beyond all that we ask or think, according to the power that works within us,

Let's look at this scripture through the filter of 'how far is God's ability to do things'? What is left outside of His reach? If we are far more abundantly, and beyond all, what is left? This is an amazing scripture because of its crazy redundancy. When we consider God's capability, it's far more, it's abundantly, it's beyond, it's beyond all. So we see that this is what's available to the believer. We're supposed to be a people who are joyful, who are rejoicing, who are excited, who are full of energy, who are shouting, who are praising, who are extolling the greatness of our God and talking about His mighty deeds! But are we doing this, is this what you experience in your life and in your church?

I can't imagine why in the world people would want to have anything to do with Jesus if we, as believers, are no different from them. If we suffer from the exact same things that have them down, why would they come to us for answers? I love Christians, however, many still come to church with bitterness, unforgiveness and anger in their hearts. Many wonder, where is God in my trial? I can't help them because God is waiting for them to give Him their bitterness, anger and unforgiveness so that He can replace it with Joy! The truth is, it's easier to be bitter, it's easier to be angry, and it's easier to not forgive. Why? Because it's easier to justify how we feel. When we tell ourselves over and over why we're justified to feel how we feel, we can't even imagine what it feels like not to feel this way. So what we end up doing is holding onto the unforgiveness, and that unforgiveness keeps us from the blessing of God. God is waiting for us to release that unforgiveness at the cross so we can be released. God wants to care for us, but He needs this to happen at that deeper level. God looks at us and says, "You are holding yourself in bondage, but there is a freedom available to you." It's that simple.

There is a freedom for us, but guess what? That freedom is harder than holding onto the bondage. Since it's easier to be angry, we have to decide to let it go and say, I'll no longer hold on to the anger and bitterness toward that person, I'm letting it go, I'm becoming free. But we need to also be aware that it often seems harder when we let go because what the enemy wants to do next is remind us of our past or our sin.

Hebrews 4:1, references salvation, but also applies to how we use our faith:

> Therefore, let us fear if, while a promise remains of entering His rest, any one of you may seem to have come short of it. For indeed we have had good news preached to us, just as they also; but the word they heard did not profit them, because it was not united by faith in those who heard.

Wait, what? Paul is talking about those who have heard and are united in faith and entered into rest. It's important to note that there IS a rest available. For those who have faith, they get to enter that rest, but for anyone who falls short of that rest, it is because they did not step out by faith; they did not believe and therefore did not enter the rest that was available to them. In order for us to be released from that anger, bitterness and unforgiveness, from that misery, we must have faith in the word of God. We have to believe that we can be set free. We have to believe that we can get past what a father or mother did to us. We have to believe that we can overcome the way our spouse treated us. We have to believe that shame and condemnation are from Satan and are not from God. We have to believe that God is for us and that He is not against us. We have to believe that God has a plan to prosper our lives and not to harm us.

We have to believe that the Lord will fight for us and that, when we resist the devil, he will flee from us. We have to believe that when we confess our sins, He is faithful to forgive.

Believers, we love the cross, but too often we do not leave our problems *AT* the cross. We want to feel the shame and condemnation of the sins of our past mistakes, and we say, "Jesus, you are not worthy to carry mine. I will carry it myself." So we walk around feeling condemned because Satan has convinced us that we're not forgiven. God puts our sin as far as the east is from the west. And Praise God, its farther than the north is from the south! See, if we go around the earth to the north, we eventually go south again. But if we go around the earth to the east, we never go west again, we just keep going east. Our sin is as far as the east is from the west, and it never ever comes back again, God brings it to His remembrance no more. It's time for us to believe that we are forgiven and walk in a forgiven state!

We have to believe that we can be delivered from any addiction, and we have to believe that we can make righteous decisions! And when we make righteous decisions, it opens the door for God to bless us. This is what we're talking about when we're talking about being filled with the Spirit. God created us, and He created our emotions. They are not a trick that the devil threw in later. No, God created us *with* emotions. But this is important to know, God even created the enemy, the one that's attacking us, the one that fell like lightning from heaven. The God who created me and my emotions also created the enemy who attacks me. If He cannot help me, what chance would I have of surviving? In other words, who is better equipped to release me from the bondage of the enemy and my emotions than the God who created them both and knows and loves me?

Don't be filled with wine; be filled with the Spirit of God. If the very Spirit of God lives in us, why is the enemy getting a hold of us? The very Spirit of God lives in me and lives in you! We have everything we need to rejoice! We have everything we need to have peace! And we have everything we need to walk in blessing! We have everything we need to overcome our past, and we have everything we need to walk confidently through this life. Why? Because the almighty God, the author of Love, the omnipresent creator of the universe, the Alpha, the Omega, the holiest of Holies, the consummate deliver, the faithful Father, the compassionate, comforting, ultimate overcomer lives in us!

So when we look at intoxication and we say, okay God, why? Why did you compare drunkenness to being filled with the Spirit? It's because when a person is drunk, they don't act normal. Listen, we did not get set free from bondage to be average! I don't know about you, but I did not get saved and set free from that sin that so easily besets me so that I could just be apathetic! What he's saying is that you do not want to be filled with drunkenness and waste your life. You want to be filled with *His* Spirit. There's a joy, there's a rejoicing, there's a shouting, and there's a whole different normal that comes on us because God is not delivering us to set us back to average! He delivers us so that we can walk in freedom and rejoice, so that we can praise the mighty works of God!

So this is what's happening to us, Christians: We believe that God has the authority, the power, the love, the grace, and the mercy to set us free. But when He does, we don't know how to Rejoice! Joy has been stolen from the church, and it's been replaced with dignity. Wow, did I just say that? YES I DID. Hey, listen to me. What is said about crazy, jumping up and down charismatics–there're drunk! Why, because our deliverance is more important to us than our dignity. The joy of our salvation gets stolen from many by pride, and yet the scripture says; the joy of the Lord is my strength! It is not *MY* joy. It is *HIS* joy that becomes our strength. So I'm asking you, when the Joy of the Lord comes for your deliverance, does it look like this? (in a monotone voice) "Oh, that's awesome. That's cool. I just got set free. I'm done with that. I've been delivered from demons. Gone. Okay. I'll go to church. I'll sing a song." MAY IT NEVER BE!!

What has happened to us? Is our freedom from sin and death not worth a celebration!? See, the reason he said, don't be filled with wine, but be filled with the Spirit is because when we're filled with this Spirit, we're full of joy! We can't help but shout and praise! This is the story that he's trying to tell us and is using drunkenness as the analogy. I can't imagine why the world would want to come and sit in a building for an hour, sing songs, listen to a speaker and go home with nothing different, nothing changed.

We carry the Spirit of the Almighty God IN us! Here's what we're saying, church, if we're not rejoicing, shouting, singing, and praising the mighty deeds of God in our lives, then the enemy is stealing our joy. We must know that it is okay to rejoice! We need to enjoy our freedom! We need to shout it out! We need to praise him! We need to sing of the mighty deeds of God! We need to lift our praise and be happy people! We need to dance, laugh, and have fun! We need to enjoy what we're doing!

I can tell you what I see because I've been a pastor for a long time. I'll get an email, maybe a text, and they'll say, "you're just hype. You're trying to pump people up to make them feel better." And this is what I say to that person: "I need you to make the most of your time because the days are evil, so don't be foolish. Understand what the will of God is, and don't waste your life. And by the way, stop criticizing and let the people of God have Joy!"

HOLY SPIRIT INSPIRATION

In this chapter, we're going to look at Holy Spirit inspiration, and it's important to look at the word 'inspired' from the Greek. The Greek word for inspired is theopnyustos. It's made from two words, *theos meaning 'God'* and *pnoe meaning 'to breath'*. So in the Greek, inspiration means "*God breathed*" or "*God's breath.*" Inspiration means *God is breathing something*. There is an inspiration, a breath of God that is given to man. It's the living word of God that's exhaled into man, and there are times when I get so excited just understanding and getting revelation about this word 'inspiration'! There are times when I'm moved to tears meditating on the significance of this word and what it means for us.

Although there are many different forms of inspiration, let's start with a foundational scripture, 1 Corinthians 2:6-13. I believe this scripture provides the most practical application of how this inspiration from God works. Here it is, mapped out for us.

> Yet we do speak wisdom among those who are mature; a wisdom, however, not of this age nor of the rulers of this age, who are passing away; but we speak God's wisdom in a mystery, the hidden wisdom which God predestined before the ages to our glory; the wisdom which none of the rulers of this age has understood; for if they understood it they would not have crucified the Lord of glory; but just as it is written, things which the eye has not seen and ear has not heard, and which have not entered the heart (the soul) of man, all that God has prepared for those who love Him. For to us, God revealed them through the Spirit.

Let's review. Paul says there's a mystery in the wisdom of God, but that mystery has not been revealed to our eyes, ears, or even our soul, which is our heart. Rather, the mystery has been revealed to us through the Spirit. Now let's look at how this plays out in the Spirit. Notice the capital 'S' referencing the Holy Spirit, and when the scripture uses a small "s" in verses 10-13:

> For the Spirit searches all things, even the depths of God. For who among men knows the thoughts of a man except the spirit of the man which is in him? Even so the thoughts of God no one knows except the Spirit of God. Now we have received, not the spirit of the world, but the Spirit who is from God, so that we may know the things freely given to us by God, which things we also speak, not in words taught by human wisdom, but in those things taught by the Spirit, combining spiritual thoughts with spiritual words.

I love the simplicity of how this is laid out, that we don't hear this with our ears, we don't see it with our eyes, and we don't even know it in our souls, but there is a revelation that comes from the Spirit of God to our spirits.

When revelation comes from the Spirit of God to our spirits, we can know the things that God has for us, the things that He has freely given us. We receive those revelations, not from what we hear and see with our eyes and ears, but from what is revealed to our spirits, from the Spirit, the very Holy Spirit of God. The inspiration of God through the Holy Spirit is given to us so that we can speak words not of human origin, but of spiritual origin.

So where do we see this kind of inspiration in our lives, and how does this work out on a practical day-to-day level? We know that the Scripture is inspired, that it's the inspired word of God. 2 Timothy 3:16 tells us:

> All Scripture is inspired by God and profitable for teaching, for reproof, for correction, for training in

> righteousness; so that the man of God may be adequate, equipped for every good work.

I believe the Bible is inerrant, infallible, coherent and cohesive *because* it is inspired by God; it was literally breathed through His Spirit into human writers. If we were to study these 66 books, realizing that the scripture occurred over a period of 1500 years with 40 different writers, it would be impossible for man to do something with this many writers over this period of time with the kind of consistency and coherency that the Bible has. It would just be impossible, and part of the confirmation that the scripture is inspired by God is the consistency of the story all the way through. The coherency of the message, how it all fits and works together, with so many prophetic declarations made early on that are later fulfilled throughout scripture, it would be impossible to do all that without inspiration!

Let's also look at revelation, which is when something that was hidden becomes known. The difference in revelation and inspiration is that revelation is "what" is revealed, and inspiration is "how" it is revealed. When something is revealed to us, something that's a mystery, something that's of God, something that comes through the Holy Spirit to our spirit, that revelation is amazing and shows us about the coherency of the Bible. In other words, the more we learn, the more we see how it all fits together. We learn something new in this book, and all of a sudden what we learned now makes something else that we never understood make sense. We move forward, learning more and more of how it all fits together, how everything in The Word and in The Kingdom fit together, often through revelation. We eventually reach the point where we cannot deny the inspiration of God with something that fits together as coherently as these books do. It's amazing to watch it roll out, and there are many inspirations in addition to The Word.

There are gifts of the Spirit that are inspiration gifts, in other words, God breathed gifts. These gifts that we operate in come directly from the throne, or indirectly through the Spirit to our spirit. There's a gift of prophesy, which is divine information given to us about future events. There's a gift called a word of wisdom, which is a divine thought providing an application for something that lies ahead. There are words of knowledge, which is information we receive, that we should not know, that could have only come to us by divine intervention. There is a gift of tongues and interpretation; these are words given in a spiritual language that can be interpreted into our language. The information distributed in these gifts are a direct communication from Holy Spirit to man.

There are two types of words given to man. When you see "word" in scripture, sometimes it's logos in the Greek. Logos means something that's already stated, something that's already written. Sometimes we look at the scripture, by itself, and say it is the logos word. But by a stricter interpretation of what logos means, we see that it means anything that has already been defined or anything that has already been stated. It includes anything that's already said. Next, there are places in scripture where the "word" is rhema in the Greek. And rhema means what is currently coming out of the mouth of God, what was spoken in a moment, what is being said now.

An example of an inspired rhema word in the Bible would be in Acts 8:29:

> Then the Spirit said to Philip, "Go up and join this chariot."

and Acts 10:19:

> While Peter was reflecting on the vision, the Spirit said to him, "Behold, three men are looking for you."

and Acts 13:2:

> While they were ministering to the Lord and fasting, the Holy Spirit said, "Set apart for me Barnabas and Saul for the work to which I have called them."

In these situations, the people were receiving rhema words. They were not repeating a written text or finding out this information was already stated sometime before they heard it. A rhema word is a word which is currently being spoken.

I believe a question in Christianity today is, are rhema words also for today, or were they only in the scripture, making them rhema words then, but logos words now. I see in a lot of Christianity today, there is only belief in the logos word, but not the rhema word of God. Those who do not believe in the rhema word of God do not believe that God speaks to us today, and that the only current inspiration is the logos word, words that have already been spoken. But the reality is that we see rhema words today through the gifts. We cannot have the spiritual gifts today and not believe in the rhema word, because they are all fresh rhema words. Interestingly, the logos word was originally a rhema word before it became a rhema word, then it became the logos word; and now when we read the logos word, it's a fresh rhema word for us today. And this is very important to note, rhema words will always, always, always be consistent with the logos word. They cannot and will not ever be in conflict.

The level of communication between the Holy Spirit of God and the spirit of man is one of the greatest honors that we have as a human. It's astounding that the God of all creation would choose to communicate directly with us. Few things will bring our Christian walk more life than knowing that we heard from God, directly from God. When we get a word directly from Him, it's something we can trust, something we can believe in. We know it's truth because it was delivered directly to us by God, and it resonates with us personally. But there's also a warning in the Bible, there's a warning about the inspired rhema word, and where the word comes from. There's a warning about watching for a false inspiration word.

In Thessalonians 2:1-4:

> Now we request you, brethren, with regard to the coming of our Lord Jesus Christ and our gathering together to Him, that you not be quickly shaken from your composure or be disturbed either by a spirit *(small 's')* or a message or a letter as if from us, to the effect that the day of the Lord has come. Let no one in any

> way deceive you, *for it will not come* unless the apostasy comes first, and the man of lawlessness is revealed, the son of destruction, who opposes and exalts himself above every so-called god or object of worship, so that he takes his seat in the temple of God, displaying himself as being God.

Paul is saying that we need to be careful because we can receive words that are not inspired by God, he says let no one deceive you. These words may be from a spirit, but not from the Holy Spirit of God. If one teaches or delivers words that are logos only, without rhema interpretation, they may not receive the full revelation of the word, or could misinterpret. Remember, the Holy Spirit will never speak of anything unless He hears it from the Father. The word of God delivered through teaching and messages must be taught AND received through the Holy Spirit. Sometimes colleges and even seminaries that teach the logos word, may just be delivering letters, or "epistles," but not the inspired word of God; one might even receive doctoral information that is not from God. If the word taught or received is not God breathed, it may have a false inspiration.

So how do we know the difference? There's a thing in every believer called discernment (not talking about the gift of discerning of spirits), which is knowing the difference between what's of God and what's not of God, in our spirit. A false word or an uninspired word is not in agreement with the word of God in our spirit. A false word is in conflict with scripture. It will not be in agreement with the character of God, and this is huge in our understanding of God and His character. We need to be watching for things to be in alignment with His character. Sometimes God will do a new thing, and we have to know if that new thing is inspired or not. The only way we can know is by asking if it comes in alignment with His character and in alignment with our spirit, because any of these words must to be in agreement in the spirit of a Spirit-filled believer. One of the most important tools we have as believers is an alive, regenerated spirit to discern spiritual things. Corinthians tells us that as believers we must spiritually appraise things.

We know as believers that there are times when we hear things about God, about faith, and about the spiritual realm, but something doesn't set right inside us. There are times when we think, "This does not feel right to me, maybe it's even disturbing, something's not right. There's something in that word that is not in sync with the character of God and I know it in my spirit." It might be pleasing to man, but we know if it's not in the spirit it's a false inspiration, it's deception. We must appraise in the spirit what is of God and what is not, because it's the enemy's intent to deceive.

I believe true inspiration is the genesis, or origin, of the word of God and the Spirit of God together. Inspiration comes when the word of God is released by the Spirit of God. When the Spirit of God breathes a word, it is inspired, and words can only be inspired if they are breathed of God. Anything that God breathes is an inspired word, and in that very breath, the word of God is delivered by the Spirit of God. This is a miraculous thing, that moment of recognizing that the God of all eternity, the creator, is about to breathe something into us. When the word of God is breathed, everything that is of the Spirit of God is in alignment and harmony with the regenerated spirit in us. It's a weapon, a tool, and a gift, knowing in our spirit that the word is in alignment with God or not.

The born-again spirit will always find joy and peace in the inspired word of God. Even if that word is a discipline, the born-again spirit of man will receive it as a blessing. In other words, "God, you may be convicting me right now. You may be confronting me about my sin, but I'm receiving it as a blessing because I know it to be truth. I know that I'm receiving it in love because I know You want what's best for me and You will correct me in love and I will receive that in my spirit because I know it's inspired." The spirit of man responds to the Spirit of God as Father.

1 Corinthians 2:14:

> But a natural man does not accept the things of the Spirit of God, for they are foolishness to him; and he cannot understand them, because they are spiritually appraised.

The natural man cannot accept the things of God because he's not using the spirit that's alive within him to appraise what he's hearing. He sees and hears in the flesh, taking things at face value because he doesn't have a regenerated spirit to know what's of God; and when the spirit of man appraises Holy Spirit, there is unity. Creation occurred the moment the very breath of God, the inspiration, came into man; this was the impartation of a Holy God into His creation.

The magnitude of this when it concerns the breath of God into man is the most intimate of connections. When a word from the Spirit of God is received in the regenerated spirit of man, there is harmony, cohesion, an understanding and a joy, because apart from creation, inspiration of God's rhema word is the most intimate moment between man and God. The Holy Spirit of God coming to the alive spirit of man is connection. The divine acknowledges the created; and the created responds to the divine with anticipation, one of the most amazing moments in our lives, when we know that God is speaking to us. I don't know about you, but I long for it. There's something in me that goes day-to-day saying, "Will it be today? Is there something you're going to say to me today? Can I possibly get a word? When will it happen?" I can live off of that word for a month. When it happens, I know we've connected. He's talking to me, and it's awesome!

I believe that the spirit of man finds a remembrance of its origin in the breath of God, a remembrance of it's origin.

Titus 3:4-7:

> But when the kindness of God our Savior and *His* love for mankind appeared, He saved us, not on the basis of deeds with which we have done in righteousness, but according to His mercy, by the washing of regeneration and renewing by the Holy Spirit, whom He poured out upon us richly through Jesus Christ our Savior, so that being justified by His grace we would be made heirs according to the hope of eternal life.

We are regenerated. The word paliggenesia in the Greek means a new birth, a new creation, a re-creation of what we were. When we are regenerated in the spirit, the Holy Spirit now has a place to dwell, to communicate in us. Once my spirit is brought to life, my spirit is regenerated and washed by the Holy Spirit so that it can become alive. There is now an opportunity for the Holy Spirit to dwell, as we can see in Ezekiel 36:26-27:

> Moreover, I will give you a new heart and put a new spirit *(small 's')* within you; and I will remove the heart of stone from your flesh and give you a heart of flesh. I will put my Spirit *(capital 'S')* within you and cause you to walk in My statutes, and you will be careful to observe My ordinances.

God says, I'll put my spirit within you and cause you to walk in my statues, and you will be careful to observe my orders. Let's look at this a little deeper; we receive a fresh, regenerated spirit so that the Holy Spirit can dwell within us. The Holy Spirit needs a regenerated, new creation to abide in. In going deeper and looking in Genesis 8, Noah is on a boat; and the entire world is under judgment. The flood was the judgment of God over all the earth, and the Spirit was sent out in the form of a dove looking for a place to rest. But it could not find a place to rest, because judgment was on the earth. However, once the judgment was removed, a new creation was formed, a new life, a new tree, a new olive tree, and the Spirit found a place to abide. This is really important to understand; when our judgment is removed by Christ, a new creation springs up in which the Spirit can come and abide.

So, what does this mean? The spirit of man longs for the breath of God to restore the relationship that he originally had with God before sin. This is why we are filled with so much joy and peace upon receiving a word from God, because it's a refreshment. It's a restoration back to our origin, back to the place where we originally communicated with God. And that inspired word of God we received through the Holy Spirit, becomes life to us. Let's look at John 6:63:

> It is the Spirit who gives life; the flesh profits nothing; the words that I have spoken to you are spirit and are life.

In context, Jesus has just said to the disciples, you must eat my flesh. You must drink my blood. And with that, many left him saying, that's just weird, that's just too bizarre, we can't go there with you, Jesus. Sorry, we don't know what you're talking about. And in turn Jesus says, you are missing the point because you're not spiritually appraising. You are looking in this conversation at the body, in the flesh, and it is supposed to be a spiritual conversation. Life comes when you consume the spiritual meaning of the words in your spirit. You receive them as spiritual terms and you understand what it means to eat his flesh and drink his blood. It's not a physical act at all.

Do you remember when Satan is tempting Jesus in the wilderness? Satan says, you're hungry, you haven't eaten in 40 days, and there are rocks here that you can eat. You have the power, Jesus, so why don't you turn that rock into bread so you can eat? And Jesus says, man does not live by eating alone. He doesn't live by the physical consumption of bread alone. Now listen to what Jesus said, He says, but man lives by every word that "proceeds" out of the mouth of God. Now that's deep when you think about it, because he didn't say man lives by everything written down in the word of God, not everything that "*proceeded*" from the mouth of God. He said man lives by what "*proceeds*" from God's mouth, *what is actively coming out of His mouth at the moment.* What is being said now, in the moment, is what man thrives on. In my spirit, I know that when God is speaking, I feel alive. The inspired words of God that breathe into our lives give us life. If God is not breathing over us now, in this moment, then we're limited to the flesh; and in the flesh we do not understand what life is.

What is life without the breath of God? It is flesh, just simply human, compared to the life God is currently speaking, which is an eternal relationship, a connection in the spiritual realm. Inspiration is when the things that the eye hasn't seen and the ear hasn't heard, which haven't even entered the heart of man; these are things that

God has prepared for us, for those who love Him. For to us God revealed them through the Holy Spirit, for the Holy Spirit searches all things, even the depths of God, so that we may know the things freely given to us by God, which things we also speak, not in words taught by human wisdom, but those taught by the Holy Spirit. Inspiration is the realm where the eternal touches the mortal and joins it to the everlasting kingdom of life. Let's repeat that, inspiration is the realm where the eternal touches the mortal and joins it to the everlasting kingdom of life. Inspiration is an open portal between heaven and earth, where words are released from God, and the spirit of man responds. Inspiration is that moment when we realize there's an external force that's driving everything we see, think and feel. Inspiration is the rain that falls on the seed, and without it there can be no growth. Inspiration is the breadth of God over the dry places to bring them to life.

It's why Ezekiel is told in Ezekiel 37:9-10:

> "Prophesy to the breath, prophesy, son of man and say to the breath, 'Thus says the Lord God, "Come forth from the four winds, O breath and breathe on these slain, that they come to life."'" So I prophesied as He commanded me, and the breath came into them, and they came to life and stood on their feet, an exceedingly great army.

Breath, in Hebrew, Ruach, means the Spirit of God, the very breath and Spirit of God. We have talked about the Old Testament being a physical picture of what we need to see in the spiritual, in the New Testament. Here Ezekiel is told to prophesy to the Spirit of God, that it might blow over these dry bones and bring them to life. In the same way that we receive the Holy Spirit when we believe so that we can be brought to eternal life, we become a great army because inspiration is that breadth of God; and when the breath of God enters man, it brings life! We become an inspired people, a people full of inspiration, a people who inspire others because the Spirit of God has breathed into us for the purpose of bringing life.

You may be thinking, I don't even understand what you're saying; you might even be thinking it's a bunch of foolishness. If that's true, the reason you believe it's foolishness is because you're not spiritually appraising it. To understand this, it must be spiritually appraised, and to spiritually appraise it, you must have your spirit regenerated. To have your spirit regenerated, you have to understand what Christ has done for you. You will never understand how you can be free from your bondage until you begin to spiritually appraise things, and you cannot spiritually appraise things until you put your faith in Christ so that you can be regenerated before God. It is the beginning of inspired communication. If you're still working in the physical realm, I challenge you today to believe in what Jesus has done so that you can understand things in the spiritual realm.

HOLY SPIRIT REVELATION

Lets talk about the Holy Spirit revelation. By definition, revelation is the divine or supernatural disclosure to humans of something related to the human existence, our world.

So in essence, something that is hidden from us gets revealed to us. That's what revelation is, the revealing of something hidden. We've already talked about inspiration, which is the very breath of God, that very touch between the eternal and the mortal. We talked about it and defined it this way: inspiration is the realm where the eternal touches the mortal and we are joined in the everlasting Kingdom of God. It can come in many different ways, the very breath of God, and the very touch of inspiration. So inspiration is the breath of God or the vehicle by which revelation is given. So now I want to talk about some of the ways the revelation of that inspiration happens. I think the Holy Spirit can do this in many ways, but He lists some gifts that He gives, gifts that we can receive revelation through. These gifts are listed in 1 Corinthians 12. You're probably very familiar with this scripture, but lets look at it again, 1 Corinthians 12:1-3 says:

> Now concerning spiritual gifts, brethren, I do not want you to be unaware. You know that when you were pagans, you were led astray to mute idols, however you were led. Therefore, I make known to you that no one speaking by the Spirit of God says, "Jesus is accursed," and no one can say, "Jesus is Lord," except by the Holy Spirit.

I think this has confused a lot of people. We talked about the regeneration of the spirit so that the Holy Spirit can come and dwell in man's spirit. So let's think of that in context of this scripture, that you cannot speak by the Spirit of God if the Spirit of God has not regenerated your spirit, so that the Spirit of God can dwell in you. But with this regeneration you can speak by the Spirit of God. So let me say it another way, you cannot speak by the Spirit of God if the spirit of God has not brought back to life and regenerated your spirit, so that the Spirit of God can dwell in you, so that you can speak by the Spirit of God. That's why this scripture says, therefore I make known to you that no one speaking by the Spirit of God says Jesus is accursed, and no one can say Jesus is Lord except by the Holy Spirit. There has to be an indwelling of the Holy Spirit in order for you to speak by the Spirit. Let's go to verses 4-7:

> Now there are varieties of gifts, but the same Spirit. And there are varieties of ministries, and the same Lord. There are varieties of effects, but the same God who works all things in all persons. But to each one is given the manifestation of the Spirit for the common good.

Common good, remember that phrase. Now let's look at 8-11:

> For to one is given the word of wisdom through the Spirit, and to another the word of knowledge according to the same Spirit; to another faith by the same Spirit, and to another gifts of healing by the one Spirit, and to another, effecting of miracles, and to another prophesy, and to another the distinguishing of spirits, to another various kinds of tongues, and to another interpretation of tongues. But one and the same Spirit works all these things, distributing to each one individually just as He wills.

Now lets look at something important in this whole conversation as it concerns gifts. If you miss verse seven, you will miss the understanding of what gifts are. Verse 7 says that *these gifts are given for the common good*. In other words, *the gifts are given in order to enhance the common good of the body*. So if the gift is enhancing only the individual, it is not a gift. For the gift to be exercised, it must enhance the common good of the body. This is how we know when the gift is being used, when it is ministering to the common good of the body.

And it lists here what we will call some of the revelatory gifts. These are gifts given for the edification of the body, gifts that are information from heaven, being given to humans, for the common good. These gifts are: the distinguishing of spirits, a word of knowledge, a word of wisdom and prophecy. I have covered prophecy in another chapter, so now I want to talk about these other three revelatory gifts.

The first one is the distinguishing of spirits. With distinguishing of spirits, one is made aware of the presence and the work of a demonic spirit(s) and angelic spirit(s). But let me clarify, this is not discernment. I think in the body today, there is a lot of confusion that there is a "gift of discernment." There is no gift of discernment, it's not listed in scripture. There is not a "gift" of discernment. If you look up the definition of discernment, you'll find it's the ability to judge. Now hear this, the vast majority of people who say they work in discernment actually work in a critical spirit. They call it the gift of discernment, but there is no gift of discernment. They actually just want to critique, and they call it discernment. I'm not saying discernment is a bad thing. I think there is legitimate discernment. And it can actually work in your life, because if it can be used properly, it's not a bad thing.

However, lets look at an example in scripture of the distinguishing of spirits. In Acts 16:16-17, Paul actually exercises this gift. What's happening here is that there is a woman that comes forth while he's traveling and ministering, and she is following him around and shouting out things that sound like good things.

> It happened that as we were going to the place of prayer, a slave-girl having a spirit of divination met us, who was bringing her masters much profit by her fortune-telling. Following after Paul and us, she kept crying out, saying, "These men are bond-servants of the Most High God, who are proclaiming to you the way of salvation."

Now, I don't know about you, but most people wouldn't see anything wrong with that at all. Isn't that what Paul is, a servant of the Most High and he's proclaiming the way of salvation? So you may not understand why this is a problem, but if you look in verse 18 it says:

> She continued doing this for many days. But Paul was greatly annoyed, and turned and said to the spirit, *(notice he did not turn and say to the woman, he said to the spirit),* “I command you in the name of Jesus to come out of her!” And it came out at that very moment.

Now I want us to think about what's happening here; the evidence of what was going on seemed very positive. Here's somebody following them around and saying, these are servants of the Most High God, and they are telling you the way of salvation. That should be a good thing, right? But Paul knew something wasn't right, something wasn't right in his spirit. As a matter of fact, he became annoyed at her talking about how wonderful he was. He knew that it was not of God and that it was demonic. He was given a revelation that these words, although sounding positive, were actually demonic. And through the Holy Spirit, he knew this was not holy.

I believe many of us actually experience this, we're just not quite comfortable identifying what it is. Have you ever been around somebody that talks really good about God, but it's like something is just not right? They say good things and right things, but there's something inside of you that just goes, “ick!” Let’s look at what this is.

We have a body, we have a soul, and we have a spirit where the Holy Spirit dwells. If we're born again believers, what happens is, the Holy Spirit, through our spirit is talking to our soul. So our soul hears something, and the Holy Spirit is saying, that's not right. The Holy Spirit releases it to our soul, which makes our body stress level raise because something inside us is not in alignment. The Holy Spirit is telling our spirit, “She's saying good things, but it's not righteous.” Our soul is saying something is not right about her because that's what I'm hearing from my spirit. And your body is saying, "I'm getting annoyed here. I'm getting annoyed and I don't even know why, but something isn't right." That's the process of the distinguishing of spirits. So Paul goes through this process with this woman and delivers her from the demonic spirit.

Lets look at something about the person who is under that kind of demonic oppression, the one who is speaking and seemingly saying good things. They will argue with you that they are of God. Why, because, they are being deceived by the demonic spirit. So they will be saying good things like, "Oh no, no, no, Paul, I'm all for you, man. You're the guy. You're of the most high and you're proclaiming the way of salvation." But she was deceived, and Paul recognized it and cast the demonic spirit out. Why? Because, he has appraised the situation in the spirit, he appraised what he is hearing through his ears and receiving in his soul and saying something isn't in alignment here. He distinguishes it as evil and he cast it out of her.

Now let's look at the next revelatory gift, the "word of wisdom." What is a word of wisdom? It's a divine answer, a given solution to a particular issue in the moment. It's the perfect solution that just comes to you. To help clarify how this word of wisdom comes about, it might be helpful for me to describe how I might see it happening in today's language. I think of a word of wisdom as that, "slap you in the head moment." It's that moment where you "drop the mic, and walk away." It's that "YES" moment where something has been spoken that is irrefutable. It's such a solid truth that nobody has anything to say after you release it. Let me show it to you in scripture; we'll look in John chapter 9. Here is what is happening; Jesus has found a man who has been blind since birth, and he has healed him, and it confuses the Pharisees. They are saying to the healed man, how did you get healed? Let's call your parents and see if you were ever even actually blind. We need to find out if you were blind from birth. Who is this guy that healed you? How did he do it? And they keep questioning the guy over and over. The healed man is kind of getting fed up with the questions because he keeps telling them, I don't know who the guy is, but he walked up and he told me and BOOM, now I can see. But in John 9:30, this is how the interaction goes.

> The man answered and said to them, “Well, here is an amazing thing, that you do not know where He is from, and yet He opened my eyes. We know that God does not hear sinners, but if anyone is God-fearing and does His will, He hears him. Since the beginning of time it has never been heard that anyone opened the eyes of a person born blind. If this man were not from God, He could do nothing.

The Pharisees are stumped. And as a matter of fact they respond, “Oh, you're all sinners! Just get outta here!” They literally have no reasonable response. This word of wisdom is irrefutable. They recognize that there's no way Jesus could have healed him unless Jesus was from God. And so the evidence in front of them is just kind of a “slap you in the face evidence” and so the Pharisees have nothing to say.

I'm reminded of things like when Jesus said to the Pharisees, as they gather around the woman who committed adultery, “Let he who is perfect cast the first stone”, and they all just walk away. Why? Because a word of wisdom was delivered. It sinks into their soul and they recognize, “That's truth. I can't do anything with that. I'm done.” It’s a divine moment where everyone just says, “You know what, that's truth right there.” And here's the beauty of it, if it comes out of you, you don't know where it came from because the truth is you don't know why you just decided to say that. But when you said it, it stopped everything. And you recognize, I just got used by God to deliver a divine truth, that was a word of wisdom. Now everybody's stumped that it’s just truth.

How do I know a smart or a knowledgeable input from a word of wisdom? How do I know the difference in somebody who is just wise and has good things to say? How do I know the difference in a word of wisdom from that kind of intelligence? The word of wisdom is irrefutable. You can't contest it. There's no way around it. It just sits there like a granite pillar. And the vast majority of the time, you would not have expected it to come from the person who said it. Not because the person who said it is not intelligent, but because it comes unexpectedly.

The next revelatory gift is called the word of knowledge. So some people are confused about the word of knowledge. They think it's the capability to gain knowledge. They believe you could be gifted to gain intelligence. That is not it at all. You cannot obtain a word of knowledge from studying. You cannot have knowledge that is naturally obtained and it be a biblical word of knowledge. A word of knowledge comes through revelation from God. It's a supernatural piece of given information for the common good. What does that mean? It means you know something you shouldn't know. You know something that there was really no way for you to know. And what you know is going to benefit someone else.

With a word of knowledge you can walk up to a man and say, "Your wife asked you for a divorce last night, didn't she?" And he breaks down in tears. He breaks, because he knows it was the last thing she said before they went to bed last night. And the wife doesn't know the person who just told him this so he could not have heard it from her. But this guy just walked up and said it because he got a word of knowledge from the Spirit.

Why do I need a word of knowledge? Because when a word of knowledge is released, the recipient knows you had no way of knowing it, and that it must have come from God. So if you have something that came from God, you have the opportunity to speak into someone because you're obviously hearing from God. So now all of a sudden the man is listening because you know something you should not have known. Now you have his attention and the opportunity to minister to him. Now you may have the opportunity to share the gospel with him.

You hear Jesus use it when he tells the woman at the well, "You've had five husbands and the one you're living with is not your husband." Now, that is a word of knowledge. Jesus also said to Nathaniel, "I saw you when you were under the tree before you even came here." This is a direct example of a word of knowledge in scripture, and this happened to Philip also. In Acts 8:26, Philip has been told there is a eunuch who is on the road to Gaza, and he is reading out of the book of Isaiah. Philip is told "I want you to go talk to him." The Lord spoke to Philip saying, get up and go south to the road that descends from Jerusalem to Gaza in verse 29. Then the Spirit said, go up and join this chariot. Philip could not have known that the guy was traveling from Jerusalem to Gaza. He could not have known that he was in a chariot. He could not have known that he was reading the book of Isaiah, but the Spirit released it to him. He got this word of knowledge, and he went and led the eunuch to Christ.

The beauty of these kinds of gifts is when we recognize that they're not from us, that they are gifts of the Holy Spirit. They are gifts to us to be able to minister to the common good in The Kingdom. There are two very important things to remember. First, the gifts are given by the Spirit, and I believe that every believer can work in all nine of these gifts. I believe that at the point in time when you need it, He will release the word of knowledge. He will give you the distinguishing of spirits at that point in time when you need it. You might prophesy, you might have a word of wisdom whenever you need it in the Kingdom of God. The second thing is, if you don't recognize that they are for the common good, you will miss their use completely. But I would be remiss not to issue a caution when operating in the gifts, the trap of pride can step in. One might find themself saying, “Hey, I get things from God, let me show you,” and it becomes about you instead of being for the good of the person receiving it. So when these gifts are used, the common good is fruit in the Kingdom of God. Let me say that again, when a spiritual gift is used properly, the common good is fruit inside the Kingdom of God.

Those are three regulatory gifts. Being able to see and distinguish an evil spirit or angelic spirit, having a word of wisdom and having a word of knowledge. But I want to talk about it from a little different aspect. I want to talk about how it relates to us in our relationship with Holy Spirit. Listen to these scriptures that I think are helpful to us in better understanding this.

In John 14:26, Jesus says this to his disciples:

> But the Helper, the Holy Spirit, whom the Father will send in My name, He will teach you all things and bring to your remembrance all that I said to you.

Acts 8:29 is about Philip and the eunuch:

> Then the Spirit said to Philip, Go up and join this chariot.

In Acts 10:8-20, Peter's having a vision that he's supposed to go meet a guy named Cornelius. He doesn't exactly know what it is about. It's a sheet with animals, but he's being given a message and it says:

> While Peter was reflecting on the vision, the Spirit said to him, "Behold, three men are looking for you. But get up, go downstairs and accompany them without misgivings, for I have sent them Myself."

He has a word of knowledge that three men are downstairs coming for him and a prophetic word that he's supposed to go with them.

Acts 13:2:

> While they were ministering to the Lord and fasting, the Holy Spirit said, "Set apart for Me Barnabas and Saul for the work to which I have called them."

Acts 21:11:

> And coming to us, he took Paul's belt and bound his own feet and hands, and said, "This is what the Holy Spirit says: 'In this way the Jews at Jerusalem will bind the man who owns this belt and deliver him into the hands of the Gentiles.'"

These are amazing scriptures! When you think about it, really amazing conversations are going on where the Spirit is saying, wrap this belt around his feet. The Spirit is saying there are three men downstairs. The Spirit is saying, I want you to go meet these people.

The Spirit is saying to him, go and find this chariot that's on its way to Gaza.

This is my question, what makes us think that the revelations from the Holy Spirit came to them differently than they would come to us today? Think about it, how is the revelation from the Holy Spirit accomplished in these scriptures? What makes us think that they had a different system than we do? In other words, did Paul, Peter, the Apostles, Philip, and everyone in the New Testament after Jesus's resurrection have a different kind of communication from the Holy Spirit than we have today? Is there anything in scripture that says the Holy Spirit related to them in a different way than he will relate to people in the future? No, it's the same system! It's the same Spirit!

So, I think when we read these stories, we believe that somehow something was different. We believe that maybe Holy Spirit showed up in some form in front of them and spoke to them audibly in some way that they understood. And they were able to learn and obey the revelation because of the interaction they had face-to-face with Him. Listen, they had the same word of knowledge that we have today, the same word of wisdom, the same discerning of spirits, and the same prophetic word. The Holy Spirit did not talk to them differently than he talks to us today. They did not have a special clarity that we do not have. They did not have a special communication system that we don't have. They had the same alive spirit in them with the same indwelling Holy Spirit in them. The same Spirit that worked and led and talked to them, works and leads and talks to us today, and in the exact same way he did with them!

I don't know if you're getting this, we hear the Holy Spirit in the same way today. I think what happens is, we read these scriptures and we attribute something going on for them that's not going on for us. Saul and Barnabas are sitting there and they hear, "these two guys need to be sent out." The Holy Spirit did not step into the room with bright lights and say, "Guys, I'm Holy Spirit. Good to meet you. I want you to get those two guys and prepare them to get ready." So we say it was easy for them because that must be how the Holy Spirit communicated with them, but that is simply not how it happened. We act like if we were alive in those days, we could follow the voice of the Spirit, because He was different then. Why is being alive in those days different than being alive these days? The Holy Spirit has not changed.

Let me show you a scripture that might help, Acts chapter 15. This is what's happening, Peter has already gone to Cornelius, and the Gentiles have now been adopted into Christ. Peter goes back to the Apostles and says, "Man, I don't know what to tell you, but God told me to go meet with them. And when I went to meet with them and I started sharing the Gospel, the Holy Spirit came down and they started prophesying and speaking in tongues, just like us. So I baptized them, and I now know that God wants them in the family of God." And so the whole group gets together and they start asking questions. They want to know, do we need to circumcise the Gentiles too, because we're all circumcised? We're not sure. So they send this information to what we call the Jerusalem council, and in Acts 15 they're trying to answer these questions about what to do now that Gentiles are coming into the Kingdom of God, and James makes the decision.

James says, you know what? We just need to give them a few simple rules, we don't need to circumcise them, we just need to tell them not to eat meat that was sacrificed to an idol. We need to tell them to abstain from blood and the things that are strangled, and we need to tell them to abstain from fornication, just these simple rules are all we need to give them. Just tell them that, and then he says, you know what we're going to do? We're going to put that in writing, and we're going to send it out with two guys and they're going to go into the Gentile areas, and they're going to have a document to give them. But I also want them to explain it to them, they need to hear how we got to this decision and you guys are the ones to do that, so I want you to go and explain it to them.

So James is sending them out, but look in Acts 15:27-28:

> "Therefore we have sent Judas and Silas, who themselves will also report the same things by word of mouth."

In other words, we're sending you, Judas and Silas, with our written document of the decision we've made, and we're sending them so that they can give it to you by word of mouth. They will explain what our document says.

Now look at 28:

> "For it seemed good to the Holy Spirit and to us to lay upon you no greater burden than these essentials."

I don't know if you saw that, but he just said it, "seemed good to the Holy Spirit and to us." Like, we were talking to the Holy Spirit, and it seemed good to the Holy Spirit to just give them a few rules. And so the Apostles said, "You know, this seems good to us too. Let's just give them a few rules." It seems so casual, this conversation, "it seemed good to the Holy Spirit and to us" to tell you that you just need to abide by these two or three rules. It's an interesting conversation that they're having with the Holy Spirit, that the result "just seemed good" to both of them. Apparently, they discussed this with the Holy Spirit and they came to an agreement.

It's almost like the Holy Spirit was giving His opinion and they agreed His opinion was the best. Like it says in John 16, the Holy Spirit said, "Let me guide you into the truth." He probably said, "You know what would be good, what would be good is that you don't go out and say, get them all circumcised. That might turn them away, just giving them a bunch of rules. So what you want to do is, you want to say, hey, stay away from this, stay away from that and stay away from this as well." So they all agree and say, "You know what, that seems really good, why don't we tell them that?"

So what happened to us? Why do we struggle so much in hearing from Holy Spirit, and why do so many believers think they can't or don't hear from Holy Spirit? I believe that most of us are waiting for a 'miraculous experience, like a glorious light to shine in our bedroom or something', and that would be 'it', so we have lost the ability to just have a simple, intimate relationship with Holy Spirit because we're looking for something big. He is often that still small voice, who speaks to and interacts with us in so many and even subtle ways.

See, the Holy Spirit is the same today as he was in the first century. The revelatory gifts he gives us are the same ones that the Apostles operated under. The Spirit gave them words of knowledge, words of wisdom, distinguishing of spirits, and the prophetic word, so that they could be guided into all truth by that revelation from the Spirit. If we look in John 16:13, notice Jesus said he will speak and disclose to us. To disclose means that something that's covered is being uncovered. He will give us revelation. He will speak to us and he will give us revelation.

Can you imagine being in your morning prayer time, and when you're done, calling a friend and saying, "You know, I was praying this morning and the Holy Spirit said, it seems good to me to call you up and encourage you today. So I'm calling you to encourage you today because it seems good to me and the Holy Spirit. So I just want to encourage you today." What a conversational relationship they had and what a conversational relationship we can have with Holy Spirit!

It is after all, the God of the universe connecting with me, this little nothing of a man. I think we believe He is so powerful, so miraculous, and so mysterious, that it's hard for us to believe He just wants to talk with 'us'. Listen, the Holy Spirit is not in an ethereal cloud that surrounds us with a thundering applause. He is not a pop in-and-out, Holy Ghost. He is not measuring our worthiness to decide whether to speak to us or not. He is not waiting for us to become good enough to talk to Him. The very times we feel most unworthy, like we just don't have our act together, is the time when He's most often speaking to us. Why? Because, He wants to help us, guide us, mature us and teach us.

So in John chapter 16:13:

> But when He, the Spirit of truth, comes, He will guide you into all the truth; for He will not speak on His own

> initiative, but whatever He hears, He will speak; and He will disclose to you what is to come.

This is important to hear, Jesus tells them that the Holy Spirit is coming to guide them into all truth. And whatever He hears, He's going to disclose to you. And it's important to look at these words: The Holy Spirit will guide you into *all truth*. This doesn't mean the Holy Spirit will dictate the rules, make decisions for you, or that He will provide every answer for you; but He will guide you into the truth. It's almost like a teacher–student relationship. Holy Spirit, you want me to not only learn, but you're going to guide me into it in a way that I can understand and grasp. I'll be able to apply it because you didn't just give me a rule that I have to then figure out how to use. Holy Spirit, you said you would guide me into the truth and if we don't believe that we can be guided in the same way as the disciples, then we'll never have those gifts unfold in our lives like they did with the disciples. They just won't be opened up to us, and we won't see and understand them. He, Holy Spirit, will guide us into the revelatory, word of knowledge, word of wisdom, and distinguishing of spirits while bringing to our remembrance what Jesus said. What is there to teach me? Plenty! By the way, John 16 also says the Holy Spirit has a purpose in our life. It's to convict us of our righteousness. It is so huge that we learn that we are being convicted of how right we are before God, that we have the "right standing" that we have! He convicts us of our righteousness.

The scripture says that He's here to guide us into truth. That's not always an instant revelation, it's a process of being guided. See, what a guide does is, He knows the destination and He knows the best way to get you there, so he walks us through the path to get us to that destination. The Holy Spirit is guiding us into truth. We have to have some foundational understanding to grab bigger things, so He will guide us with the foundational things.

He wants to be a helper to us. His goal, His purpose, scripture says, is to be the Helper. He wants to help us. He wants to teach us these things; He wants to bring to our remembrance the things that Jesus said. How can He do that if He doesn't talk to us? Maybe it's time we put down the intimidation of the Spirit and pick up the intimate relation of the Spirit. He wants to love us, help us, teach us and guide us. And do you know what? Sometimes, He wants things to just "seem good" to you. Stop waiting for that cataclysmic, foot of the bed, bright, shining thunderous voice with sounds and surrounding angelic hosts playing harps and shofars and just listen to Him speak.

I know some of you feel like you haven't heard from Him in a long time. You may say, I don't think I've ever heard from Him like everyone else does. I want to guide you into something here. The Holy Spirit dwells in your spirit and is releasing information to your soul according to 1 Corinthians 2. So we're going to have to hear it in our soul, not through our ears. We need to listen for the Holy Spirit's words more in our soul, through His Spirit, than through our ears. Words *can* come that way, but I don't believe that's the way He gives revelation. I believe when the scripture says, "*He said to them*," he was speaking to their souls through their spirits. What I'm going to ask you to do is get quiet, and I'm going to give you a question to ask the Holy Spirit. And after you ask that question to Holy Spirit, I want you to be silent and listen to what you hear through your soul, through His Spirit.

Now you may hear something that isn't from the Holy Spirit, but let me tell you how to know if it's from the Holy Spirit or not. Holy Spirit will never, ever, ever work in condemnation, ever! It's not who He is, so He would never use it. He does not condemn; He convicts. He says, "You can be better, I've got more for you, I'm going to release more to you, we can go beyond this!" He does not say, "Man, you blew it, you're a mess." That's condemnation, and if you're hearing that, it's not Holy Spirit. Holy Spirit is going to speak to you and He's going to encourage you. He's going to convict you, and He's going to motivate you to move forward. He's going to say the thing you need to hear in your soul at that moment. Some of you may think that this is risky, but I promise you, it's Him, and He wants to talk to you. He wants to speak into you, and He's been waiting. I don't even know how you might react; you may be so touched, or you may break out crying. If you do, that's ok, that's normal, just cry! You may feel very warm inside, or even butterflies, this is normal, because He's an emotional God, and He speaks to us in emotions! Just be open to how He wants to speak to you, and receive it and embrace it. His voice is always edifying and not condemning; receive His good words and feelings over you when He speaks to you!

Here's the question you're going to ask. You're going to ask Holy Spirit, "Do you love me, Holy Spirit, do you love me?" You're going to ask that question and then you're going to be silent and still and wait for what comes to you, and we're going to believe it is from the Spirit, unless it's condemnation. Are you ready? Just close your eyes and ask the question. "Holy Spirit, do you love me?"

For some of you it will come quickly, and others may say, "I didn't hear anything." Here's my suggestion. Ask again. "Holy Spirit, do you love me?"

My Prayer For You:

Father God, I thank you for your love for each of us. I thank you that you love each one of us individually and completely, and I thank you for sending the very Spirit of God to help us, teach us, guide us, and give us revelation. I thank you for revelation, where you personally encounter each of us, and revelation for the common good. Thank you Father that we're a people who want to hear from you, so I know that you will minister, and I know that you will meet and speak to each of us in our souls, and you'll meet us in our quiet place at home. We are going to be a receptive people. Our ears are open to you, Holy Spirit, just like when the Apostles were told to get up and go, we will get up and go because we've heard from you. Holy Spirit, just like the apostles assembled somebody and sent them out because you said to send them out. We will hear those words from you and we will send out. We will go to the highways and the byways because you told us through revelation to go to the highways and byways. We will recognize that you are talking to us the same way that you talked to them, and we want our responses to be the same as theirs. So Father, we love you. Holy Spirit, we love you. Jesus, we love you. And in your name Jesus, we welcome the Holy Spirit in our lives. Amen.

HOLY SPIRIT VERBALIZATION

In this chapter we're going to talk about tongues. If you're reading this and you were not raised in a charismatic environment, some of what I say may be a struggle for you, but we're going to look at this in scripture. If you were raised in a charismatic environment, some of what I say may be a struggle for you as well, because again, we're going to look at this in scripture. The topic of tongues is widely misunderstood in the church, and it creates division and fear. With that, a lot of God's people, and tongues specifically, are widely silenced in the church due to religion and control.

One reason this is such a difficult topic is that there seems to be almost directly contradictory scriptures about it in the Bible. Things like, tongues are for the common good; yet tongues are speaking to God, not to man. Things like, tongues must have interpretation; yet Paul says, I pray in tongues, and whose prayer requires interpretation? Jude says, pray in the Spirit all the time; yet there are scriptures that say tongues will cease. And then Paul says, I wish that you all spoke in tongues, and do not forbid the speaking in tongues. So, we need to take a deeper look at tongues. What happens today in many churches is, we cherry pick the scripture that is most comfortable for us in our church. We go through scripture grabbing the "clubs," (that's what I call them), the clubs we can use to keep people in line with our beliefs, where we're going, and how we want 'our church' to be. But there's a real danger, such a danger in looking at a scripture and not referencing the character of God when we read it, because what happens is, we'll take a scripture out of context and miss what He has for us because we overemphasize or underemphasize something in a particular scripture, and not considering the whole scripture.

Let's look at an example of cherry-picking scripture. Do you know that neither Jesus nor Paul could have been a Deacon in the church today? Because when we look at the scripture, a deacon must be the husband of one wife, and since neither was married, they would not be able to serve as Deacons in our churches today; and we would have missed the opportunity to have Christ serve as a Deacon in our churches today! So, we have to look at the context, what is He teaching us instead of just pulling a line out of scripture and trying to use it.

What I want to do first is to clarify in advance that some things I'm going to share may cause some tension within you, but I'm asking you to stay with me to the end because I will support everything I'm saying in scripture. The first point I would like to make is that tongues exist today for the purpose of praying. There are also tongues with interpretation for today, which are a gift of the Spirit for the common good of the church, but it's important to note that these are *two different things* in scripture.

Let me state that again, "tongues" are for prayer, and the gift of "tongues with interpretation" are for the common good of the church. I also believe that all believers can pray in tongues. If you don't speak in tongues, don't stress about it, but I believe we can all pray in tongues because our spirits have been regenerated. Our spirits have been brought to life; they've been brought into The Kingdom. We were once dead in our trespasses and sin, but now we're made alive in Christ. Our spirit, which has been brought to life, prays. On the other hand, not everyone has the gift of tongues and interpretation.

Secondly, in this conversation it's important to remember that we have a body, a soul, and a spirit. Our body is the physical part of us, our soul is our mind, will and emotions; the things that make me, me and you, you apart from what we can see. Then we have our spirit that was breathed into us by God. Our spirits are the ruach breath of life into man so that he could become a living soul. Adam and Eve had a spirit, and that spirit is what died because of sin in the garden. When man is born in sin, he's under the prince of the power of the air. And so, his spirit is not alive, but when he comes to know Christ, his spirit is brought to life. So, we have a spirit in us, and scripture calls it the spirit of man. The scripture shows us that the regenerated spirit can pray. The spirit has a language if you will, so let's jump straight into scripture with these premises and see what we learn.

Let's start in 1 Corinthians 13. Let's start with the group that believes tongues have ceased. This miraculous thing has ceased, so there are no tongues for today. Let's look in scripture at what is used to teach cessation. Cessation is the belief that these gifts have ceased, therefore the word cessation, or ceased. I don't believe it's an accurate teaching. 1 Corinthians 13:8-13 says:

> Love never fails; but if there are gifts of prophecy, they will be done away; if there are tongues, they will cease; if there is knowledge, it will be done away. For we know in part and we prophesy in part; but when the perfect comes, the partial will be done away. When I was a child, I used to speak like a child, think like a child, reason like a child; when I became a man, I did away with childish things. For now we see in a mirror dimly, but then face to face; now I know in part, but then I will know fully just as I also have been fully known. But now faith, hope, love, abide these three; but the greatest of these is love.

This is one of the scriptures used to say that tongues don't exist anymore. Some say we don't have tongues in church today because this scripture says that prophecy and tongues and knowledge, at a minimum, will cease. But remember it says they will cease when the perfect comes. Clearly, when the perfect comes is when these things will cease. The argument has been used that the word of God is "perfect." Clearly, the word of God is perfect in every way. So, with this belief, when the perfect word of God, the Bible, the New Testament we have today, when it came into being, there was no longer a need for these gifts. There are two things to think about when considering this belief. First of all, what we currently have as a New Testament, these 27 books that have been assembled, these were not assembled and finalized as good for teaching, reproof, rebuke and all of those things for the believer until 397 AD in the

Council of Carthage. So this Bible was not even assembled as the 27 books we have today for over 360 years. So those who would say, well, when the Bible came, it was the perfect word, therefore we don't have tongues anymore. That didn't happen until 400 AD, so we would have to believe that tongues ceased around that time and that the completion of the New Testament Bible caused them to cease. But lets look at three distinctions in this text that prove this line of thinking is not an accurate interpretation. Are you ready? Paul is the same writer of both Corinthians and Hebrews. He wrote one as a Jew to the Jews, and one to the Greeks. We remember that Paul said to the Jews, I become as a Jew to the Jews, and so on. So, although the books have a different writing style, we believe Paul wrote both. In the book of Hebrews, there are five times that Paul refers to *Jesus* as the perfect and in Hebrews 5:8-10:

> Although He was a Son, He learned obedience from the things which He suffered. And having been made perfect, He became to all those who obey Him the source of eternal salvation, being designated by God as a high priest according to the order of Melchizedek.

Hebrews 7:28:

> For the Law appoints men as high priests who are weak, but the word of the oath, which came after the Law, appoints a Son, made perfect forever.

Hebrews 2:10:

> For it was fitting for Him, for whom are all things, and through whom are all things, in bringing many sons to glory, to perfect the author of their salvation through sufferings.

Hebrews 5:9:

> And having been made perfect, He became to all those who obey Him the source of eternal salvation,

Hebrews 12:2:

> Fixing our eyes on Jesus, the author and perfecter of faith, who for the joy set before Him endured the cross, despising the shame, and has sat down at the right hand of the throne of God.

So the first evidence that the perfect is not the New Testament Bible, and that the perfect is Jesus, is that the writer has been referring to the perfect as Jesus. This is our first indication that the phrase 'when the perfect comes' is referring to when Jesus returns.

The second proof to examine is in 1 Corinthians 13:10-12:

> But when the perfect comes… For now, we see in a mirror dimly, but then face to face;

No offense, but I can't actually be face to face with my New Testament Bible, whereas I can be face to face with Jesus. It's a reference to the fact that we're going to be face to face with Jesus one day.

The third proof is that it says, "now I know in part, but then when the perfect comes, I will know fully just as I've been fully known." I'm going to be real honest here, I've had the Bible all my life, and I've been reading it since I was probably six years old, but in the 50 years I've been reading it, I don't fully know. But this scripture says that when the perfect comes, if it is the scriptures, I'm going to fully know. That has not been true for me. The New Testament has mysteries in it that I know are still there waiting for me, so I don't fully know although I have the New Testament. But when Christ comes, I will fully know: prophecy will be fulfilled, knowledge will be exposed and tongues will cease. Why? I believe it's because communication is going to return to the way it was in the garden. When God walked with man in the garden, there was a communication, a conversation, a language that was present until the Tower of Babel split that language and sent it all over the earth. I believe there's going to be a restoration for all men of the language they spoke in the garden. But the point is, according to 1 Corinthians

13, 'the perfect' cannot be the New Testament Bible because it doesn't fit the description Paul is talking about.

However, it totally makes sense that Jesus is the perfect that comes. In other words, I will not need to speak in tongues when Jesus returns because we'll have a pure language. We'll not need prophecy, it has already been fulfilled, and there is no reason for the gifts to continue after Christ has returned.

To conclude the reference: "*when the perfect comes*" *is talking about when Christ returns*. See Paul says right now in this earth, I'm a child. I only know things partially; but then when I'm mature, I will know things fully. Therefore, I can put away the things that I used as a child, the gifts! I won't need these anymore because I fully matured in Christ at His return. Does this make sense?

The second argument used for these gifts having ceased is something called Apostolic dispensation. So lets clarify what this means. There was a time when the Apostles, who were appointed by Jesus, were on the earth. Some argue scripturally that the Apostles started and launched the church, therefore, they needed miraculous abilities in order to capture people's attention. This one I could argue against all day long, because the Holy Spirit convicts today, and he could have convicted the same way He did before with or without the miraculous.

The argument is that because the Apostles could work in those miraculous things, that when the Apostles were gone, that dispensation ended and the miraculous no longer happens. Here's the problem with that line of thinking. First, for a dispensation to end, another dispensation has to begin. When the Abrahamic dispensation ended, there was a Mosaic dispensation. When it ended, there was a Davidic dispensation. So what dispensation began after the Apostles died? None. It was the church age from the time that Christ was risen and returned to heaven until now. How do we prove that? In Matthew 28:19, Jesus is talking to the Apostles and this is what he says:

> "Go therefore and make disciples of all the nations, baptizing them in the name of the Father and the Son and the Holy Spirit, teaching them to observe all the things that I commanded you; and lo, I am with you always, even to the end of the age."

Notice he says, teaching "them" all the things that "I commanded you." What did He command them to do? He commanded them to heal the sick, to cleanse the leper, to raise the dead and to do the miraculous (Matt 10:8). So, all of the things that he taught them, he said, "Now I want you to go teach the nations." He didn't say, "I'm commanding you to tell them to do all the things I've commanded you, except that miraculous stuff, except the gifts stuff, except tongues." He doesn't say that. He says, teach them all that I've taught you. And it's important to note that when Paul was teaching in the book of Corinthians about gifts, he was teaching *the church* how to use them, not the other Apostles. Paul was teaching *the church* members about using the gifts. So why would he be teaching church members how to use the gifts if they were only for the Apostles during their time? It wouldn't make sense.

So, I believe that tongues are a relevant gift for today, but no doubt there is also a lot of confusion about it, and this is what I want to do. I want to take the "scary" and the "crazy" off of tongues so that we can look at it. Because I think we need them in the church, and I think we need to stop looking at this thing as something weird and something odd. We need to figure out how this is supposed to work in the church and what the value and purpose is, because it has been so messed up and confused in the church. And isn't it just like the enemy to want to mess up and confuse important things of God?

So as we read scripture, we see that all tongues are a language. Tongues are language. If we went and did a study of how many languages are on the earth right now, there are 6,500 identified languages. If we were to rattle off a bit of each of these 6,500 languages, just saying a sentence or two, they would all be very different. They would each be unique. Some would flow, some would sound choppy, others would have great inflection, and others would sound monotone. So, there are many different languages and types of language, but everyone communicates with a language. Robert Morris, one of my favorite pastors, demonstrated it this way. He has a two-year-old granddaughter and he went and sat with a phone and videoed his two-year-old granddaughter, as he asked her a question. He said, "What's does that look like to you?" And she just began saying, "blah ah be may too eesh kay." In other words, something that sounded like gibberish. And he asked further, "I know, but what are you going to do after that?" She responded with, "a kah blee an see otta boo." Again, responding in what seemed to make no sense to Robert. Robert's point was that although he did not have a clue what she was saying, he knew that she did. I know there's a language going on there, he said. I just don't know '*her*' language. There are languages we hear that may sound like gibberish, but they are not, they are languages. They are communicating something even though 'we' may not understand them.

So, let's go look at scripture to find out why. 1 Corinthians 12:7-10:

> But to each one is given the manifestation of the Spirit for the common good.

There is a manifestation of the Spirit given for this purpose, for the "common good;" In other words, so that we all are edified, so that we all are 'built up'. These manifestations are given for the common good. Now Paul is going to give us a list of some of these manifestations.

> For to one is given the word of wisdom through the Spirit, and to another the word of knowledge according to the same Spirit; to another faith by the same Spirit, and to another gifts of healing by the one Spirit, and to another the effecting of miracles, and to another prophecy, and to another the distinguishing of spirits, to another *various* kinds of tongues, and to another the interpretation of tongues.

Now these are gifts. They are manifestations of the Spirit, given for the common good of the church! This is going to be real important in a minute. These are gifts given for the common good of the church. And when it comes to tongues and interpretation, they have to go together. What good would the gift of tongues be if it was never interpreted? And what good would the gift of interpretation be if there were no tongues to interpret? So, the gift of interpretation always goes with the gift of tongues because it's interpreting what is being said in tongues. We see those two things together and Paul begins to talk about this whole conversation in 1 Corinthians 14:1-5:

> Pursue love, yet desire earnestly spiritual *gifts*, but especially that you may prophesy. For one who speaks in a tongue does not speak to men but to God; for no one understands, but in *his* spirit he speaks mysteries.

Now this is where some of the confusion begins. This is what Paul just said. When one speaks in a tongue, he's not speaking to man, he's speaking to God, and it's his spirit (man's spirit) that is speaking mysteries, because no one understands what his spirit is saying. Confusing, right? How can it be for the common good if man is talking to God and its all a mystery? Well, let's dig in and see.

First, a major point is that his spirit is speaking, not his mind or his soul. Paul didn't say a man speaks out of his thought process, he says it's out of his spirit. Do you remember earlier we made point about the body, soul and spirit of man? Here he said his spirit is speaking, it's not in the thought processes. So, if you don't believe you have a spirit, this is a real struggle for you because your spirit speaks mysteries. If you have not been born again, if you have not been baptized in the spirit, you may wonder, "Well, why am I not speaking from my spirit yet?" And it may have something to do with the status of your spirit, and if it has been regenerated yet or not. But it says no one will understand what we're saying from our spirit.

Now look at verse 3:

> But one who prophesies speaks to men for edification and exhortation and consolation.

What is Paul saying? If you are prophesying, you're speaking in the recipient's language so you can edify them, you can build them up, you can encourage them.

But verse 4 says:

> One who speaks in a tongue edifies himself; but one who prophesies edifies the church.

What? He speaks mysteries from his spirit, but it edifies himself. The speaking in tongues edifies the person who is speaking in tongues? What does edify mean? If you look up edifying in the Greek, it's often referenced with building a house. You're building, upon building, upon building. You're edifying. You're strengthening. You're putting more and more onto it to make it stronger and stronger. So what he's saying is happening to the person who *speaks the tongue*, *his spirit speaks mysteries,* and it edifies the person speaking in tongues. It makes them stronger and stronger. For those of you who do not speak in tongues yet, when I pray in tongues, it makes a difference in my soul. In other words, I can feel a strength. I know that I'm declaring something, and I know that I'm breaking something. I know I'm building myself up by praying in this language.

Then it says, but the one who prophesies edifies the church, that's the common good. Next Paul says, I wish that you all spoke in tongues. Remember, he's telling the church in Corinth, not the Apostles. *He's telling this to the church*:

> Now I wish that you all spoke in tongues, but *even* more that you would prophesy; and greater is one who prophesies than one who speaks in tongues, unless he interprets, so that the church may receive edifying.

Here he says there's a greater thing that's happening in prophecy than tongues, but why? Why does he say that? Greater is the one who prophesies than one who is speaking in tongues unless he interprets so the church could be edified. In other words, what he's saying is that when you prophesy, you're speaking in a language they understand. That's a greater deal for everyone to hear and understand. That brings more edification than speaking in tongues because they don't understand what you're saying. But he says tongues can be edifying if they're interpreted. So there is a gift of prophecy for the common good of the church, and there are tongues WITH interpretation for the common good of the church. Because tongues without interpretation does not contribute to the common good, because no one knows what is being said without interpretation.

I became a born-again believer at 20 years old. I walked an aisle when I was 8, but I understood the gospel when I was 20. I was a born-again believer, believing in the gifts of the Spirit, and even though my denomination didn't teach it, I believed in it, I just didn't understand how they worked or how to operate in them, that's all. I did not speak in tongues for 30 years. For 30 years I believed in something, but was unable to operate it. You might say, well, what's the deal? If Paul wants us all to speak in tongues, why would it be withheld? I believe for me, it was withheld for the purpose of my current church. I believe he said, I have a plan for you, and I'm going to baptize you in the Spirit and you will start teaching this stuff later in your life.

Let's review what Paul has said up until this point. If you speak in tongues, you're not speaking to men, but to God, no one will understand your tongues. Your spirit, small "s," is speaking mysteries, and when you do this, you're building yourself up. He goes on to say that unless that tongue is interpreted, it doesn't edify anybody (although it does edify you) because they don't know what you're saying. But notice that prophecy edifies others because they do know what you're saying.

Then we come down to maybe the beginning of an understanding of what is happening. Paul starts explaining that '*he*' prays in tongues. He prays in a language that edifies himself as the scripture says but is not for everyone else. 1 Corinthians 14:14-19 says:

> For if I pray in a tongue, my spirit prays, but my mind is unfruitful.

Did you notice it said, "If I pray?" So, the topic is praying in tongues, and it says, "My spirit prays." In other words, when I'm using this language, it's not my mind praying, my spirit is praying. My spirit actually has the cooperation of my body because my body is speaking out what my spirit is praying. Then it says, "but my mind is unfruitful." This is where I struggled with tongues for a long time. I would even tell my kids when I was younger, "Why in the world would God want us to pray something that we don't even know what we're praying? Who knows what we're praying, we could be praying something completely wrong, and we *can't* do that!" Then Paul goes on to say:

> What is *the outcome* then? I will pray with the spirit and I will pray with the mind also; I will sing with the spirit and I will sing with the mind also.

He is saying that when I pray in tongues, my mind doesn't know what I'm saying. What's the outcome then? In other words, what am I going to do about the fact that when I pray in tongues, my spirit is praying, but my mind doesn't know what I'm saying? Here's what he says he's going to do. I'm going to pray with my spirit and I'll pray with my mind. I'm going to sing with my spirit and I'll sing with my mind also. In other words, he's saying, since I don't know what I'm saying when I'm in the spirit, I'm going to also pray things that I know that I'm saying with my mind. Oh and by the way, I'm also going to let my spirit pray. But my spirit wants to pray even though I don't understand what my spirit is praying. So, I'll just do both. Paul says he prays in tongues and also that he doesn't know what he's saying when he's praying in tongues. Therefore, he will pray in tongues *and* in his own language.

This is a huge point! Paul prays in tongues, but he does not say his prayer in tongues needs to be interpreted. Whoa! So, he's praying in tongues, but there's no interpretation? I know that's going to throw some of you for a loop! Why is there no interpretation? Why? Because he's praying… in his spirit. Keep reading in verse 16,

> Otherwise if you bless in the spirit only, how will the one who fills the place of the ungifted say the "Amen"

> at your giving of thanks, since he does not know what you are saying?

Who are the ungifted? The ungifted are the people who do not have the gift of interpretation. You're praying in the spirit, and they don't have the gift of interpretation. They don't know when to say Amen. They won't know when because you're praying in a language they don't understand, and they don't have the gift of interpretation.

> Otherwise if you bless in the spirit *only*, how will the one who fills the place of the ungifted say the "Amen" at your giving of thanks, since he does not know what you are saying? For you are giving thanks well enough, but the other person is not edified.

He is saying, when you pray, and someone is with you, pray in the language they understand. He doesn't say go ahead and pray in the spirit and get it interpreted for them. He says, if you're with someone else, pray in their language so that they understand, they can come into agreement with you and they can say "Amen." He also does not say, do not pray in tongues; he says if someone is with you, pray in a language they understand so they can be edified.

It's important to remember the context of what he's talking about in this section of scripture, which is 'when to pray in tongues' and 'when to pray in your language'. He says, when I pray, I'm edifying myself and my mind doesn't understand, so I'm going to pray in the spirit *and* in my mind. But when I'm with somebody else, I'm going to pray in their language so that they can be edified, and so that they can join me in that prayer.

So, the entire conversation up to this point is, I pray in tongues, I sing in tongues, I'm speaking to God, not to man. This is to build *me* up. But if I'm praying with someone else, I should pray in the common language. Then he says in verse 18:

> I thank God, I speak in tongues more than you all;

In other words, Paul says, I speak in tongues a lot. I am not sure how he could have known how much each of them speak in tongues, but he said, this is what I do know, I pray in tongues more than you do.

And then there's something that happens in the next scripture that I believe has completely messed up the church on this topic. Because there's this little set of words here that changes the dynamic, it changes the direction, it changes what he's talking about. He says, I thank God I speak in tongues more than you all. Let's look at verse 19:

> However, in the church I desire to speak five words with my mind so that I may instruct others also, rather than ten thousand words in a tongue.

Say this with me, "however, in the church." Let's stop right there for a moment. Up until this point he has never said anything about "in church." He has talked about his own prayer life and when he prays in tongues and when he doesn't. And he said, if anybody's with me, I make sure I'm praying the language they can understand. Then he says, let's put all that on a shelf for a moment and talk about, "in the church," when we assemble together. 1 Corinthians 14:19:

> However, in the church I desire to speak five words with my mind *(in the language I know)* so that I may instruct others also, rather than ten thousand words in a tongue.

This is huge in this scripture! He has just changed the topic from when to pray in tongues and when to pray in the common language to what we should do in church! How is this going to work in church?

Now remember when we go back to the list of gifts, Paul said the gifts, including tongues, are for the common good. Now we're in the common crowd, in church. So how can praying in tongues be for the common good? Paul says, if he is praying in tongues, he's not praying to man, but he's praying to God. So, isn't it impossible for tongues to be for the common good? Hear me out here. *Tongues in prayer are for the edification of the person praying*. But, *the gift of tongues WITH interpretation is for the common good.* When we get into the common arena, we're talking about the gift of tongues with interpretation.

There are two different uses of tongues that Paul is referring to here, not two different languages, but two different uses. He says, I have a prayer language that I pray in tongues, and I do it in my spirit and it edifies me even though I don't know what I'm saying. But when I get into the arena of the common good (in church), we're going to speak in tongues *and* have interpretation. Let's look at this. He is going to address how to use tongues in the church. So we get to this new topic, 'instruction for the church,' and he says in verse 23:

> Therefore if the whole church assembles together and all speak in tongues, and ungifted men or unbelievers enter, will they not say that you are mad?

Let's think about this from the standpoint of what's going on "in a church service." If a person walks in, and everyone in the room is speaking in tongues, and the person coming is ungifted or an unbeliever, what would they think about what is going on in the room? An ungifted man is thinking, "I don't have the gift of tongues or interpretation, I don't know what you're saying." An unbeliever hasn't even been regenerated in his spirit to work in these kinds of things at all. So, they just hear a whole bunch of people talking in a whole bunch of different languages and they will say, these people are mad, these people are crazy! They're all together, yet they're all speaking in different languages; how strange is that!

Now let's consider what Paul is trying to teach here. If those same people walked in the door and a man got up and began to speak in language nobody understood, but a lady stood up and told us what he just said, then the two men coming in would say, "Oh wow, I get it, he speaks a language I don't know, but she knows his language and mine so she can tell me what he said." That's what Paul is saying here, he's saying that ungifted and unbelieving people are going to think it's crazy if they come in and everyone is speaking in different languages (tongues) at the same time. Basically, he is saying, don't all of you speak in tongues at once because the unbeliever and the ungifted would be confused and pulled away from the things of the Spirit. They will think the things of the Spirit are crazy instead of understanding and saying, "Wow, what an amazing gift." So, when you're assembled, tongues and interpretation go together. This is not the prayer language he spoke of previously, instead, this is what we are to use when we assemble together. Both are tongues, but when we assemble, it is tongues with interpretation. Look at vs 27:

> If anyone speaks in a tongue, *it should be* by two or at the most three, and *each* in turn, and one must interpret.

So, here Paul provides instruction for tongues with interpretation in a church service, which is straight up practical. Let's do this one at a time. If five of you are speaking five different languages, we don't know what anyone is saying, but if one of you speaks a different language and one of you interprets, we are all edified because now all of us understand what you said, then he says:

> But if there is no interpreter, he must keep silent in the church; and let him speak to himself and to God.

So here is something 'straight up,' in most churches this is the 'big club' to keep everyone in line. "If there's no interpretation you can't speak in tongues in church. If somebody speaks in tongues and there is no interpretation, we need to run them out of here, because that's not biblical!" But see, that's not a correct interpretation or application of these scriptures. I've had people leave our church, telling me they left because during worship someone was praying in tongues and nobody interpreted. It was unscriptural, unbiblical, and offensive. The problem is, their interpretation of the scripture is not correct, and they became offended over a misinterpretation and misapplication of scripture, and this is a common occurrence in the church. My response to this man was, "God bless you, keep studying." Keep studying because you're missing the character of God and the point of this entire discussion by creating a rule on it, that is religion. That interpretation of scripture is not what Paul is saying. What he's saying is, there will be tongues in church, and it needs to be done in such a way that everyone is edified, and the only way everyone can be edified is if it's interpreted. But again, that's with the *gift* of tongues and interpretation '*in the church*'.

Let's look at this another way. If we were all in worship and somebody a few seats from us had their hands up in worship, saying, "God you're awesome and I love you, and I thank you for your love for me and the way you always take care of me." If everyone was singing and participating in worship, what would you think? You would think, "That's awesome! They're praising God, they're caught up in worship, maybe they're just praying." But if someone is standing there praying in tongues, one might say, "wait, stop, stop this, there is supposed to be interpretation, you can't do that in here." I say, NO, leave them alone, they're praying, they're worshiping God, so leave them alone.

How does one know the difference of whether someone is praying in tongues, or if it's tongues with interpretation for the common good? This is how we know; if that person who is speaking in tongues is praying and not wanting everyone to stop and hear the prayer and interpretation, then they are simply praying in church. If there is a situation where the person has a word in tongues for the church, then it will be delivered in a way that the church can be edified, similarly to a prophecy being delivered publically for the good of the body.

So let's look at this, because it's really important. Paul says if someone gets up and speaks in a tongue in your church service without interpretation, he tells them to keep silent. Why? Because if there is no interpretation, then it is not for the common good! That's when he says, be silent. There is no common good happening if tongues is spoken out to the congregation but no interpretation is offered, so we need to tell that person to stop, because there is not interpretation to bring common good.

First of all, let's be practical about tongues during a church service. How are we going to know if we have an interpreter if nobody speaks out in tongues? So there needs to be a speaking out of tongues first. But once there is a speaking out in tongues, then we would ask if there is an interpretation. And if there is an interpretation, it is the gift of tongues with interpretation! Enjoy it, it's for your good and edification! Now watch, if there is no interpretation, then someone is speaking out in their "prayer language" and this is what he says to them in verse 28:

> But if there is no interpreter, he must keep silent in the church; and let him speak to himself and to God.

Notice, he says they must keep silent "in the church." But keep reading! What does it say after that?

> But if there is no interpreter, he must keep silent in the church; and let him speak to himself and to God.

Let him speak to himself and to God! Let him! Wait a minute, what was the prayer in tongues? Speaking to God, not to man. So, he wasn't telling him to stop his tongues. He specifically says, be silent and continue to pray in tongues. In other words, what you just did was not the *gift of tongues and interpretation* so it should have been *kept in the context of prayer;* it was not for the common good.

Sometimes this adds to the craziness for those who didn't grow up in a charismatic environment, who don't understand it. One might say, "Why is that person yelling out that stuff in tongues?" Paul is saying, if it's the gift of tongues, there's going to be an interpreter. And some of the craziness would go away if after they yelled it out, someone would tell me what they just said. But if it is not tongues with interpretation, and it's just one's prayer language, then Paul says, sit down, be quiet, and just keep praying. For one who speaks in a tongue does not speak to men, but to God.

So the previous conversation Paul was having before verse 14 was just Paul helping to explain tongues as a way to pray. He also said if someone is praying 'with him', he chooses not to pray in tongues. But then he says in the church it works like this. If someone speaks out, there needs to be an interpretation. If there's not an interpretation, then they're actually speaking out in their prayer language, so you can tell them to sit down because that's not the gift for the common good. But if they get up and they speak in tongues, there should be an interpretation. If there's an interpretation, that's the gift which is a blessing for the common good.

He finishes with this in verse 39:

> Therefore, my brethren, desire earnestly to prophesy, and do not forbid to speak in tongues.

Now how can a person who doesn't want tongues in the church say, don't forbid speaking in tongues? I grew up in a church that forbade speaking in tongues. The church I grew up in believed that they ceased. But for those who do not believe they ceased, I still see churches who use the "club" to prevent them from happening in a church service, and I am here to tell you that you are grieving the Holy Spirit and preventing the common good in your church.

There is also some crazy teaching out there about tongues. One of the crazy teachings is, you've got to be careful with tongues because you could get tongues of the devil. You could be speaking out evil. Go back and read what the scripture says, Luke 11:9-13:

> "So I say to you, ask, and it will be given to you; seek, and you will find; knock, and it will be opened to you. For everyone who asks, receives; and he who seeks, finds; and to him who knocks, it will be opened. Now suppose one of you fathers is asked by his son for a fish; he will not give him a snake instead of a fish, will he? Or if he is asked for an egg, he will not give him a scorpion, will he? If you then, being evil, know how to give good gifts to your children, how much more will your heavenly Father give the Holy Spirit to those who ask Him?"

Why did Jesus use a snake compared to a piece of a fish and a scorpion compared to an egg? Listen, what are snakes and scorpions in scripture? Demonic! Snakes and scorpions are symbols of the demonic. The devil is portrayed as serpent, and Revelation 9 speaks of demonic scorpions. So looking back to Luke 10:19:

> Behold, I have given you authority to tread on serpents and scorpions, and over all the power of the enemy, and nothing will injure you.

So what is this scripture saying? Snakes and scorpions represent the demonic, so if we ask the Father, He's not going to give us something demonic! If we ask the Father for the gift of tongues He will not give us something demonic! As a matter of fact, what He says is, He will give us the Holy Spirit. So, we leave it in God's hands, knowing that when we earnestly ask if we can have this language, we know we will not get something demonic because He says, if you ask me, I will not give you anything demonic. I will give you something of the Holy Spirit.

Now, I know that those of you who, like me, grew up in a conservative church environment, are nervous about how all this "tongues" stuff is going to work, so let me go ahead and make the charismatics nervous for a moment. I grew up in a Bible believing conservative denomination, not in a charismatic church. I'm not saying those are against each other, but I was sitting in my church one day and there was a movie showing on the screen. And I was asking God, "Why would you take a Church of Christ, and Baptist born and raised guy, baptize him in the Spirit, and put him over a charismatic church? Was it so that everybody can tell me how I'm doing it all wrong? The movie I was watching was called Holy Ghost, and in the movie, RT Kendall stated that there has been a silent divorce in the church between the word of God and the Spirit of God, and that in the church, those things need to be brought back together. When he said that in the movie, it was like the Holy Spirit backed up with a dump truck and unloaded it on me. I hit the floor in tears and the Holy Spirit said, "That's why I picked you."

Here is both the problem and the blessing that brings to the table, I don't really understand a lot of the charismatic traditions. But this is what I do know, there are two things that drive me right now. One is the assignment to bring the word of God and the Spirit of God back together. But inside of that assignment, number two, is helping people who grew up in the environment I grew up in accept the things of the Spirit. In other words, sometimes we need to tell the charismatic group, "Can you guys slow down? We don't know what you're doing." And we have to tell the traditional group, "Can you guys just accept that this is in the Bible and it's okay to do?"

And so, tongues becomes one of those things where the traditional group is like "….what?" And the charismatic group is like, "Oh yeah!" But I believe the charismatic group often struggles with their own traditions over what scripture says. Let's look at just one example, 1 Corinthians 14:26:

> What is *the outcome* then, brethren? When you assemble, each one has a psalm, has a teaching, has a revelation, has a tongue, has an interpretation. Let all things be done for edification.

So taken literally, this says people will come to church with a song, a teaching, a revelation or a tongue. But why is it in a charismatic environment that the only thing that receives a spontaneous delivery in a service is tongues? And why do we believe in the charismatic circles that if someone is going to speak in tongues, it's going to be a spur of the moment, out of nowhere occurrence? And that when it happens, everybody has got to stop and listen? What I'm saying is, when I read this scripture it says, some come with the song, some come with the teaching, some come with a revelation, and some with a tongue. Now here's the problem I have, either we're completely doing church wrong or what we're actually supposed to do is gather together and wait until something spontaneous happens; a song, a teaching, a revelation or whatever.

I've got a real issue with how we would have spontaneous teaching in the church. What if someone wants to give a spontaneous teaching at my church, and I don't even know if they are a visitor, and I might not necessarily even know if they were a believer. So I come prepared with a teaching. I've been studying for weeks. I come to the church service with a teaching, and my daughter, who is our worship leader, comes with songs. She has already practiced with the band and given them songs. I am not saying she cannot do something spontaneous, but for worship, we come prepared. Oftentimes someone who comes in with a prophetic word will tell me in advance, “Pastor, I've got a word this week for the church, can I give it?” Or maybe during the service they will come up to me and ask if they can give a prophetic word; if I sense a unity in the Spirit, then my response is, “sure!” Give me the word, or let me give you a mic and let’s pick the right moment to give the word. This is completely done in order without bursting forth in shouting from the congregation.

So, why do tongues need to be spontaneously delivered? Because every charismatic I've talked to says, “When somebody rips out in tongues, you’ve got to get everybody quiet so we can hear them and see if there's an interpretation.” I'm saying, why is it done that way, because nothing else is done that way and nothing in scripture indicates that tongues should be done that way. Even Jesus, when he was in the Synagogue, didn't jump up spontaneously and say, “I am anointed, hey everybody, I am anointed!” It says in Luke 4:16-20:

> And He came to Nazareth, where He had been brought up; and as was His custom, He entered the synagogue on the Sabbath, and stood up to read. And the book of the prophet Isaiah was handed to Him. And He opened the book and found the place where it was written, “The Spirit of the Lord is upon Me, Because He anointed Me to preach the gospel to the poor. He has sent Me to proclaim release to the captives, And recovery of sight to the blind, To set free those who are oppressed, To proclaim the favorable year of the Lord.” And He closed the book, gave it back to the attendant and sat down;

Jesus stood up to read, the book was handed to Him, He opened the book and read, then He closed the book, gave it back and He sat down. There is nothing spontaneous about that! So I'm asking as a non-charismatically raised person, “Why do tongues need to be spontaneous in a service? Why? Why couldn't a person with the gift of tongues come and say, “I have something I am supposed to deliver in tongues.” “Okay, let's let you deliver it and see if there's an interpretation, okay?” Because when you deliver it and we get an interpretation, it's a beautiful thing. Everybody's edified by it and they all think that's great. Wow, tongues can actually makes sense!

Now, I'm not saying it cannot be spontaneous. I think sometimes we're in a service and our worship leader spontaneously sings. They get something and they begin to sing it out. But it's in order because they are currently leading and we follow them and it's in the moment. When a person has a prophetic word, we can give them a mic and they can deliver the word so its done decently in a way everyone can hear. So, what I'm saying is, I think part of the scariness for most people who did not grow up in a charismatic environment is actually the "tradition" of how tongues have been delivered in charismatic services.

I believe tongues should be in the church, and I want to better understand how tongues and interpretations can be used in the church service, but part of what I am doing is questioning the traditional way it's been done to ask, "Why is it done that way?" For instance, part of properly delivering a prophecy is to do it decently and in order so that everyone in a large auditorium can hear it, and the same is true with tongues and interpretation. Part of the decently and in order is doing it so that everyone in a larger group can hear it and benefit.

So I'm not saying tongues can't be spontaneous, the scriptural basis for tongues being spontaneous is when a wind came in, tongues of fire fell on their heads, and they all started speaking in another language spontaneously. I'm just going to let you know, if a wind comes into our church service and there's fire on everyone's head, I'm hitting the floor because all rules are off, and God can do it however He wants to do it! I want to understand the rightful use of this gift in the church because it's supposed to edify us and we're missing out on opportunities to be edified because we're following traditions. Let me also add that spontaneity typically has a lot more freedom in a small congregation. Paul uses the phrase decently and in order, and for the most part, most people who complain about tongues complain that it is out of order. But my questions are actually more along the lines of how we can do it decently. As an example, if a person lets us know they have a word in tongues to give, wouldn't it be easier to quiet everyone and give them a microphone? Then it can be delivered decently.

Let me add one more thing to finish. This was the problem for me and I believe it's the problem for the majority of the people who don't speak in tongues. Listen, if you don't speak in tongues yet, don't stress over it. I gave up on it, and then I asked for it again, and gave up on it, and asked for it again, over a period of 30 years. Here's the thing that's the biggest problem with understanding why you cannot speak in tongues. The biggest problem is that it's not a product of your mind. Again, it is not a product of your mind. What do I mean by that? I mean, if I attempt to speak in tongues and say "somebody-bought-a-honda!" (stated humorously) I've just thought through what I'm going to say. So, what I thought to speak came from my mind, it did not come from my spirit.

So the question is, how do we release ourselves to let the spirit speak through us? Are you ready, because here is the answer: You've got to be out of your mind! That's right, that's it. You have got to be out of your mind, meaning it has to be coming from the spirit, and not the head. I know because I'm a thinker, a strategist, a studier, and this was the hardest thing for me. I had to figure out how to stop thinking and let something flow out of me? I didn't know, I really didn't know. I got baptized in the Spirit in 2013, and it was three months later, when I thought all these gifts should be here, because I got baptized in the Spirit, and I was still not speaking in tongues. So one morning I'm out on my back patio having my devotion, and I'm talking to God saying, this is supposed to be available to me, but I don't know how to make it happen. He said, "Right." It was His response to "I don't know how to make it happen," "Right."

So, I began to worship, I put on some music and I opened my mouth and a different language came out that was absolutely beautiful. But let me tell you what happens so that you can stop struggling with this. As soon as something comes out of your mouth, you might say, "This is ridiculous, I'm just doing this, I'm just making it happen." Listen, give it a chance, and let it go. Even if you think you're just being foolish, let it flow. Why? Because for me, in about two and a half minutes I was flowing in a language saying words I'd never said before in complete conjunctive sentences that had a rhythm and a rhyme and I knew I was speaking a language. I didn't even have to think about it; it just came out. It's like my spirit was saying, “You've been praying out of your mind for 30 years, hush up and give me a chance,” and the same will be for you if you will stay out of your head.

The thing to remember from this is that praying in tongues is your spirit praying. Scripture tells us that we can pray in tongues because we have a spirit that has been brought to life. We were dead in our trespasses and sin, but we have been made alive in Christ. So our spirit can, and I believe wants, to pray. And we're allowed to pray in tongues in church. It's the legalist, religious one, the ones who don't understand yet, that want to put a stop to this because they don't understand that we're praying in tongues which is not meant for interpretation.

If you don't pray in tongues yet, I know this can be a struggle. It was for me for a long time, but then God just released it and it's a beautiful thing. It's a very helpful thing, and it’s powerful. It’s warfare against the enemy, and we have a real enemy. This is what happens for me, any time I'm down, frustrated, really battling something, not knowing what to do, I pray in tongues. I will pray for about 30 minutes, and by the time I’m done, I am ready for anything! I'm happy to say I don't understand what I said, but what I've learned is that I don't need to know, I just know what it does for me, it builds me up.

This is what I want you to do if you have accepted Christ as your Savior. I want you to get in your closet, in your bedroom. I want you to get in whatever worship moment works for you, whether it's music, silence or whatever, and I want you to say, “God, how do I get this? How does this get released to me?” And when it starts to happen, stop telling yourself that it's not real, that it’s crazy. It's part of who we are, and it's biblical. It's part of what we use to build ourselves up, and it's part of our experience, it's just one of many. Prophesying is another, and so is faith, and giving, and healing. They are all different kinds of things that we operate in for the common good.

My prayer for you:

Father God, we love You, and we thank You God that we're just digging into the word trying to understand it. God, we see the benefits, and we see the way that you edify people through prophecy, and we want to see how You do it through tongues. We want to see and experience the strength that there is for us personally in our prayer time. We want to bless everyone who is a believer who does not currently pray in tongues to just step out of their minds for a moment and let their spirits pray in their private time. Thank you God, that we are just pursuing truth, that we're asking questions, God, in the holiest of ways. We're studying for better understanding. We pray that we've released some truth today, and some level of understanding that would allow us to walk in Your way. In Jesus name. Amen

HOLY SPIRIT EDIFICATION

I've decided to title this edification. I could have used prognostication, exhortation or consolation. There's a lot of "tion" words to use, but I use this one because of 1 Corinthians 14:26. Paul, in his discussion on the gifts, says this:

> What's the outcome then, brethren? When you assemble, each one has a psalm, has a teaching, has a revelation, has a tongue, has an interpretation. Let all things be done for edification.

This list of things is for the common good, for edifying the body. Edification is the building up of something. If we were to talk about constructing a house and we knew that we had to put some walls up, we would need to edify, strengthen or fortify those walls. Edification is the very thing we do to strengthen those walls. We would nail them together. We would put braces in between the studs and maybe we would put sheet rock on the outside of the studs. All of these things would be done to increase the strength of the wall, to build it up, to make it better.

To start, it will be helpful for us to look at prophesy. The scripture says that prophecy is about edification, and by biblical definition, prophecy is speaking forth by divine inspiration. In other words, something divine is being spoken forth through you. There's an inspiration, a very breath of God that's coming to you and being released by you, and it's called the prophetic. The prophetic divine inspiration from God can actually come in many different forms. I believe we often miss the prophetic because we don't realize it comes in different ways. Sometimes it can come in a dream, a prophetic dream. Other times it comes in a vision where you're just sitting and thinking, and all of a sudden you've got this picture or image. Sometimes it just lands directly into your spirit by the Holy Spirit. Have you ever just received a solid truth out of nowhere that landed in your spirit? You thought, "That wasn't from me, but it's for me, and it's a true word!" Sometimes it comes out of your circumstances, such as a friend giving you a new jacket, representing a new mantle you are to receive. It's a physical manifestation of the prophetic that's going to happen. Sometimes it's a Rhema word where God is actually speaking into you and telling you something. Sometimes it's from the Bible, from the logos word. Have you ever read a scripture and boom, it jumps out at you, and you know you are supposed to stay on that scripture, it's a word for you now, and you're supposed to meditate on that word for the time being.

My call into ministry came from a prophetic word out of the logos word of God. In other words, I read something and God said, "Read that again." I read again. "Read that again." I read it 26 times and He said, "That's for you." It took 26 times to get through to me. So basically, prophetic words from God can come in many different ways.

It will be helpful for us to look at prophecy as a whole, an umbrella view, and then drill down into specific areas. The prophetic is a very large topic and difficult to cover in just one chapter, but we'll start with 1 Corinthians 12:4-7. I believe there is something here that a lot of people miss:

> Now, there are varieties of gifts, but the same Spirit. And there are varieties of ministries, and the same Lord. There are varieties of effects, but the same God who works all things in all persons. But to each one is given the manifestation of the Spirit for the common good.

Did you notice gifts, ministries and effects? All of these are for the common good. How do we know if we're operating in one of these, when what we're doing is for the common good? But it says there are gifts from the Spirit and there are ministries from the Lord (that would be Jesus) and there are effects from God. There's actually a difference in each of these, and we'll look at that difference in scripture. They all have a different or unique purpose in the body. When it comes to prophecy itself, we'll look at the difference in the gift of prophecy vs. the ministry of the prophetic.

There are three basic types of prophetic in the scripture that apply to all of us. The first one we'll call simple prophesying. It's edification, exhortation, and consolation for others. In other words, we should all be able to do simple prophesy. We should all be able to build one another up, exhort each another, and console one another.

1 Corinthians 14:1-2 says:

> Pursue love, yet desire earnestly spiritual gifts, but especially that you may prophesy. For the one who speaks in a tongue does not speak to men but to God; for no one understands, but in *his* spirit he speaks mysteries. But one who prophesies speaks to men for edification and exhortation and consolation.

Let's unpack this a bit. He said, when you're speaking in a tongue, we don't know what you're saying. Somebody has to translate that for us. It has to be interpreted for us. But when you're speaking prophetically, you're speaking in our language and we are edified by it because we know what you're saying.

Then in verses 4-5:

> One who speaks in a tongue edifies himself; but the one who prophesies edifies the church. Now I wish that you all spoke in tongues, but *even* more that you would prophesy; and greater is the one who prophesies than the one who speaks in tongues, unless he interprets, so that the church may receive edifying.

Notice that he said greater is the one who prophesies, unless there is interpretation. So if there is interpretation, they are equal in value. He is saying, prophesying can instantly edify, but tongues must be interpreted to be edifying. So, prophesying is great. Tongues are great. But prophesying is better because we get instant edification and we don't need the interpretation.

When we look at this scripture, there's no doubt that God wants us to prophesy, and this particular kind of prophesying lifts people up, it inspires them, it encourages them. This is one way we know the Holy Spirit never condemns, because it's an inspiration and it's the very breath of God. If it's coming through us because the Spirit lives within us, and we're delivering the message from God, that message will not have condemnation, because the Spirit comes to convict believers of our righteousness. He will always tell us what's ahead in a way that brings conviction or courage. If someone says, "I believe what God wants to say is that you're really a lousy person." I can tell you that's not prophecy. It's not from God. God doesn't speak in those terms. Here's how God might put it to do the same thing with conviction instead of condemnation. "I believe God wants me to tell you today that there's so much more for you. You actually have life in your tongue and you could be using that for The Kingdom." The difference is, one brings condemnation, and the other brings a conviction to be better. That's how the Spirit speaks when it comes to the prophetic. If the Holy Spirit dwells within the believer, then speaking and encouragement should come naturally to us because what's already there is just flowing through us, and all we are doing is opening the conduit. This is why Paul says, I wish that you all would prophesy because the Holy Spirit gives every believer that capability.

The Bible also talks about another specific type of prophecy, the gift of prophecy. More than just encouraging and edifying, this is when a person with the gift gives a specific message to a particular audience.

This gift of prophecy is shown in 1 Corinthians 13:2:

> If I have the gift of prophecy, and know all mysteries and all knowledge; and if I have all faith, so as to remove mountains, but do not have love, I am nothing.

And Romans 12:4-5:

> For just as we have many members in one body and all the members do not have the same function, so we, who are many, are one body in Christ, and individually members of another. Since we have gifts that differ according to the grace given to us, *each of us is to exercise them accordingly*: if prophecy, according to the proportion of your faith.

Prophecy can be a gift, as tongues is a gift, and they are very similar. They are both messages from God, and there is a check and balance for both of them. The check for tongues is the interpretation. We know the validity of tongues is based on the interpretation, and the prophecy is measured by a prophet, which we'll explain in this chapter, but they are both a message from God delivered to help the body. Both are specifically from Him for a designated audience, and the difference is tongues needs an interpretation whereas prophecy does not. Both, I believe, are something any believer can do.

There's another category of the prophetic listed in scripture, and it's called the ministry of the prophetic. We remember the Spirit gives gifts, but the Lord gives ministries.

In Ephesians 4:11 they are listed like this:

> And He gave some as apostles, and some as prophets, and some as evangelists, and some as pastors, and teachers, for the equipping of the saints for the work of service, to the building up of the body of Christ.

I believe this is unique because the Spirit gives us gifts for the common good of the body, and Jesus gives us ministries for the building up of the body. Are you seeing the same thing? These are all for edification and the building of the church, but this one is a ministry. Some people call it an office. I like the word ministry better because I think that defines it better for us, and maybe to some degree keeps the ego out of it.

In 1 Corinthians 12:28:

> And God has appointed in the church, first apostles, second prophets, third teachers, then miracles, then gifts of healings, helps, administrations, various kinds of tongues.

Here we're talking about the ministries, the effects and the gifts. We don't really struggle with identifying pastors, teachers and evangelists, it's easy to see people who work in these ministries. We all know people who work in the ministry of a pastor, people who work in the ministry of a teacher and people who work in the ministry of evangelism, but we struggle a bit more with those who work in the ministry of the apostolic and the ministry of the prophetic. It's a little more challenging in some denominations. If you knew me personally, I work in the ministry of the apostolic, partly because God uses me to start churches, and I am in my third church plant. All three churches are still thriving, yet I also work in the ministry of the teacher. God has given me the ability to take biblical information and transfer it in a way that's easy for most to understand, so I am an apostolic teacher. We have these ministries in our churches because God puts them in the body for the building up and for the common good of the church.

These ministries are not new, and they're not just for the New Testament church. Some would say, "The five fold ministry is just for the New Testament church, it's only for the people under the New Covenant, these ministries were given with the outpouring of the Holy Spirit in the New Testament, so they did not exist before." But that's not true; if we go back in scripture, we'll see that they are in the Old Testament too. Thinking about the gift of prophesy, let's look at 1 Samuel 19. In this scripture we're going to see the ministry of a prophet as well as an example of the gift of prophecy. When we look in I Samuel, Saul is looking for David, because he's got some business he wants to take care of with David. David is actually running from Saul. He's hiding from Saul because he believes Saul wants to kill him.

1 Samuel 19:18-24 says this:

> Now David fled and escaped and came to Samuel at Ramah, and told all that Saul had done to him.

David meets with Samuel and says, "this is what Saul's trying to do."

> And he and Samuel went and stayed in Naioth. It was told Saul, saying, "Behold, David is at Naioth in Ramah." Then Saul sent messengers to take David, but when they saw the company of the prophets prophesying, with Samuel standing and presiding over them, the Spirit of God came upon the messengers of Saul; and they also prophesied.

Here are these soldiers from Saul who have come to take David, but when they get there, Samuel is presiding over a group of prophets and something very unique happens. The Spirit of God comes upon the messengers of Saul. The men who came to take David actually start prophesying! Talk about a trippy moment! They're on their way to take this guy captive, to bring him back to their King, and they get there and they start prophesying! Then Saul finds out what happened:

> When it was told Saul, he sent other messengers and they also prophesied, So Saul sent messengers again the third time, and they also prophesied.

We can see Saul's getting a little frustrated. "I keep sending my guys out to take David and bring him back to me, and they end up being prophets!" So, Saul decides to go and get David himself.

> Then he himself went to Ramah and he came as far as the large well that is in Secu; and he asked and said, "Where are Samuel and David?" And someone said, "Behold, they are at Naioth in Ramah." He proceeded there to Naioth in Ramah and the Spirit of God came upon him also, so that he went along prophesying continually until he came to Naioth at Ramah. He also stripped off his clothes, and he too prophesied before Samuel and lay down naked all that day and all that

> night. Therefore they say, "Is Saul also among the prophets?"

I don't know about you, but I think this is kind of funny because Saul's not a good guy in this story. He's trying to capture David, so he sends his guys and they all end up joining the prophecy group until Saul says enough of this, I'm going to go myself! He doesn't even get there before the Spirit of the Lord gives him the gift of prophecy. The Spirit came upon him and he begins to prophesy. This has got to totally confuse Saul. He's got to be wondering, "why am I prophesying," then he ends up on the ground naked prophesying for days.

I hope you get this–prophecy breeds prophecy! You may be thinking, "Well, I'm not very prophetic." Here's what I'm saying, "Get around prophetic people." If we get around prophetic people, the Spirit of the Lord will come upon us, and we'll get this prophecy thing figured out pretty quickly. Saul's messengers are not prophets, but the Spirit of God came upon them and they begin to prophesy. The Spirit gave them the gift of prophecy, even though they weren't in the prophetic ministry. Then the same happened for Saul.

We see this again with Moses in the book of Numbers. If we go to Numbers 11, Moses is having a rough time. He's the leader of a large group of people and they are totally wearing him out. Moses basically says, "God, I need to give up leading or you need to give me some help." God says, "you know what, I'm going to give you 70 men. I'm going to take what's on you and I'll put it on 70 men and they're going to start helping you."

This is what we see happen in Numbers 11:24-29:

> So Moses went out and told the people the words of the Lord. Also, he gathered seventy men of the elders of the people, and stationed them around the tent.

The tent of meeting is always outside the camp, and Moses would leave the camp to go to the tent of meeting to meet with God, but this time he brings these 70 out and has them surround the tent.

> Then the Lord came down in a cloud and spoke to him; and He took of the Spirit, who was upon him and placed *Him* upon the seventy elders. And when the Spirit rested upon them, they prophesied. But they did not do it again.

So here's what's happened; Moses has been the only prophetic leader up until this point. He says, “I'm kind of drowning here,” and God says, “I'll give you 70 men to help you. What I'll do is I'll take the Holy Spirit that's on you, and I'll put it upon them and they will be able to prophesy too.” And then there's this last sentence that may not make sense at first:

> But they did not do *it* again.

Why is that sentence in there? But they did not do it again. It's because of what's about to happen next. What we're about to read next is they are saying there wasn't a second anointing, there wasn't another placement of the Spirit on other men, but look what happened in their midst:

> But two men had remained in the camp; the name of one was named Eldad and the name of the other Medad. And the Spirit rested upon them. (now they were among those who had been registered but had not gone out to the tent), and they prophesied in the camp. So a young man ran and told Moses and said, “Eldad, and Medad are prophesying in the camp.” Then Joshua, son of Nun, the attendant of Moses from youth, said, “Moses, my lord, restrain them.” But Moses said to him, “Are you jealous for my sake? Would that all the Lord's people were prophets, that the Lord would put his Spirit upon them!”

Moses is saying to Joshua, “You think there are too many prophesying now? Seventy-two is two too many for you Josh? Well I think it would be great if all of the Lord's people were prophets, that the Lord would put his Spirit upon them.” Let me tell you what just happened. Moses just prophesied. He just said, I would pray that a day would come when the Spirit would be upon everybody and they would prophesy.

So in Acts 2:17-18, the Spirit comes, and they begin to speak boldly. They begin to teach, and they begin to speak in other languages. As Peter gets up to preach, he quotes the book of Joel:

> "And it shall be in the last days," God says, "that I will pour forth of my Spirit on all mankind; And your sons and your daughters shall prophesy, and your young men shall see visions, And your old men shall dream dreams; Even on my bond slaves, both men and women, I will in those days pour forth of My Spirit and they shall prophesy."

Did you see that? What Moses prophesied in Numbers 11, just happened. He says, one day God is going to pour His Spirit out on everybody because I wish that everyone would prophesy.

I'm reading Corinthians and Paul says, you guys need to pursue prophecy! You need to earnestly desire gifts, but especially that you would prophesy! I read these scriptures in the Old Testament where people were prophesying, and even the people that got near them began to prophesy, and I'm thinking the message is that we should want prophecy in our life.

Then 1 Thessalonians 5:16-20 says this:

> Rejoice always; pray without ceasing; in everything give thanks; for this is God's will for you in Christ Jesus. Do not quench the Spirit; do not despise prophetic utterances.

If we'll notice, there is a semi-colon after Spirit meaning its part of a list that follows. He's saying, do not quench the Spirit by despising prophetic utterances. Let me tell you what most believers see when they read that scripture, they say, "If someone is going to prophesy, we should not despise it. We should let them prophesy, we should be okay with it." But they never apply it to themselves, do not quench the Spirit “in you” by despising prophecy utterances “from you.” In other words, if you refuse to prophesy, you are quenching the Spirit. Now here is the rest of the list concerning the quenching of the Spirit:

> But examine everything carefully; hold fast to that which is good; abstain from every form of evil.

What this scripture just said is, do not quench the Spirit, thus despising prophetic utterances. So, a lack of prophecy in the church shows a quenching of the Spirit. This is important; if there is not a flow of prophetic words in the church, then the Spirit IS being quenched.

God's inspired revelation has to be perfect because it came from God. But here he says, examine everything carefully, hold fast to that which is good and abstain from every form of evil. How can something from God be evil? Why would we need to be careful if it's from God, shouldn't it be perfect? Here's why, because this thing called man gets involved. Man's interpretation of that inspiration can be subject to error. I saw this clearly a couple of years ago. An elder approached me and said, be careful when you give a prophetic word, that you only give what you get because if you begin to expound on it, you could take it into a different direction than what the receiver is supposed to hear. In other words, sometimes we have to be careful that what is being given is only the inspired part and not something added by us.

Then 1 Corinthians 14:31-33 tells us:

> For you can all prophesy one by one, so that all may learn and be exhorted; and the spirits of prophets are subject to prophets; for God is not a God of confusion but of peace, as in all the churches of the saints.

Let’s first take note that Paul says the spirits (small ‘s’) are subject to the prophets. In other words, the spirit of man is subject to other prophets. He also says you can all prophesy one by one. Paul is in a situation in Corinth where he's trying to explain to them that they are a little out of hand and that they need to get some order in place on some things that they do. He tells them they can prophesy one at a time, and that way they can avoid confusion. But there's also this comment about the spirit of the prophet being subject to a prophet. If a person is speaking of God, what one says needs to be confirmed by someone else, because man is in the mix. And because the scripture says that we prophesy in part, and someone else in the prophetic may have an addition to that part.

1 Corinthians 13:9 says:

> For now we know in part and we prophesy in part;

The beauty of the system is that it's the same thing as tongues. Tongues are spoken, and we know it's an inspired word of God if someone has an interpretation. A prophetic word is spoken, and someone has to come into agreement with it. It makes sense that a prophetic word would have a confirmation, just as a tongue would have an interpretation. It's not difficult to understand the validity of the prophetic when there is a check and balance, and someone other than the person giving the word validates it to ensure "man" didn't get in the middle of the communication. And the same with tongues, one person gives the tongue, and another person, the interpreter, just interprets what is said. If we speak a prophetic word, then someone prophetic would say, "I agree, I see that too, I heard that over you also. And you know what? Maybe this goes with it." Maybe there's an addition that goes with it, for instance, it could be a balance, a clarification, a refinement of the word. God wants to make sure that man is not in the way, so He puts this checkpoint in prophecy and tongues.

It shouldn't be confusing. When we think of teachers and the ministry of the teacher, how often have we listened to a teacher and then go back to check that scripture against the way it was taught, or maybe listen to another pastor or check with someone else and say, the teacher explained it this way, does that make sense to you? It's a check and balance for the responsibility of teaching. This is how we learn and grow as believers, we should never take anyone's word for anything without thoroughly checking it out, and yet even with teaching, people often don't, yet they'll 'dis' the prophetic. But it's the same way with the prophetic; it's a ministry that has, in essence, a balance put in place so there'll be some confirmation of what was said.

The danger I see most often with the prophetic and this balance of the word, is the people who go somewhere to get a word. "I'm going to this conference because I need a word for me. I'm going to be in church today, and I'm going to go up front and raise my hands, I'll even cry if I need to so they'll see I need a word." What happens with these people is, they 'get a word' and they run with it. "This is it! That's what they told me. I'm in, let's go!" They head out in a direction and there's no confirmation of it at all. I'm not saying it was wrong, I'm saying sometimes we can hear something different than what was said and we need a prophetic balance on the word. We need someone else to say, "yes, I see that too," so now we've got a check and balance. Words take time to meditate on and consider, they are not always for now or in the moment, they often roll out over time, and may be confirmed by additional future words.

We'd be remiss if we talked about prophecy and didn't talk about the fact that there are false prophets and false prophecies.

If we go to 2 Peter 2:1-3:

> But false prophets also arose among the people, just as there will also be false teachers among you, who will secretly introduce destructive heresies, even denying the Master who bought them, bringing swift destruction upon themselves. Many will follow their sensuality, and because of them the way of the truth will be maligned; and in *their* greed they will exploit you with false words; their judgement from long ago is not idle, and their destruction is not asleep.

What did he just say? He said the beauty of having more than one input is you can find out what is false because false prophets actually desire their own fame, their own sensuality. They are going after their own lust. It's about them and the fact that they gave a word and you are respecting them as prophet. They are in a false prophet mode.

False prophets also want to manipulate you with their words. Sometimes people will give you a prophecy over something they already know about you, something they know you're struggling with that they found out second hand. And then they will come and say, "I perceive that God wants you to know that you're struggling with this." And they already knew it in advance. That's a false prophet. They're manipulating you for their own gain. They are not proclaiming an inspired word. The beauty of this scripture is that in the end God says their judgement from long ago is not idle. It's coming, and their destruction isn't asleep. In other words, God is saying "I'll take care of them." So we just need to look for that balance, that confirmation.

Prophecy is a beautiful tool for the common good of the church. Paul says, you should want to prophesy, to go for it, seek it, desire it. Why would we want to shut down the very channel of communication that was meant to deliver an inspired word from God for the common good of the church? Why would we want to stifle that any more than we would want to stifle good sound teaching? Paul says open that bag up, let that thing loose. We want it to be active in our lives and in the body of Christ–His Church. So my question is, are we seeking to prophesy? What evidence is there that you are earnestly pursuing prophecy?

In 1 Corinthians 14, three times Paul says, pursue love yet earnestly desire spiritual gifts; but especially earnestly desire that you may prophesy. Now I wish that you all spoke in tongues, but even more that you would prophesy. Therefore, my brethren earnestly desire to prophesy and don't forbid the speaking in tongues. Our instruction in the word of God is to especially pursue prophecy. We need to pursue prophesying because it was given to the church to edify the body, to encourage the body, and to console the body during trials. Paul says we need this in the church. You need it! Why would we not want to go to someone in the church and build them up? Why would we not want to say, "I have this beautiful word from God that's going to encourage you today." Why would we not want to be hungry for the opportunity to grab you out of darkness and bring you into the glorious light of God? Why would we not rush in to lift you up? Why would we not be grateful for the chance to let you receive a word from God? Is there any better place to build someone up than in the church?

One of the things that's going wrong in our society today is that we have become a people with stories of victimization. We become popular by having a more traumatic story than another person. We basically say, "Hey everyone, my life is difficult and my life is harder than yours." Our words have become victimization, and we have forgotten how to speak words of life. We have forgotten how to speak declarations of truth that bring about edification, that build one another up. Why? If I know what it's like to be down, would I want you to stay down when I have the opportunity to give you something from God that would lift you up and build you up? In this world of victimization, in this world of medical diagnosis, in this world of political separation, this world of racial division, this world where the enemy seeks to divide us, why would we not want to prophesy to one another? Why would we not want to build one another up? Why do we not want the opportunity for the God of the universe to speak to your heart through a brother or a sister in Christ.

1 Thessalonians 5:11:

> Therefore encourage one another and build one another up just as you're doing.

Our speech has gotten critical. We can't turn on the TV without a fight, argument or debate whether among talking heads or in families. There are debates about everything. Our words are negative, critical, and we don't agree and encourage. Many of God's people today are suffering from depression, anxiety, boredom and sorrow because we've lost the desire to speak life. What would it be like to come to church and everybody you speak to is building you up saying, "Oh my, you're amazing! God has plans for you! He told me something great is around the corner! You're just a phenomenal singer! I love the way you worship! The glory of God is just all over you!" Then we can walk away from church dancing and shouting,

"Oh yeah, I've been to church, I've been to church, I've been in the presence of God, I've been with Jesus!" What would it be like to the world if the church was a place where you just felt great when you left because everybody there was saying "You look good! That cancer is not going to stay. We're going to get that to leave you right now!" Instead we say "how's your week?" And the response is "It's been hard. Everything is going wrong. The dog ate a whole bag of food by himself and now he's sick. And I got this pain in my foot and my boss will not give me a raise." It's sad to see.

What an opportunity we have because the truth is, we're just in a society that likes to talk about their struggle and does not want to talk about their joy. Most people want somebody to talk to because they're struggling. What happened to the believers that wanted somebody to talk to so they can pour into them, so they can build someone up, so that person can have a better day?

If we were all sowing encouraging words, what would we be reaping? We should be in a place where everybody is encouraging us. Why? Because I am encouraging everybody and building them up, and they are building me and others up, because I was building them up. See how it works, it's so circular, but how do we do this? How do we pursue prophesy? What can we do to get in the mode, to develop the habit of pursuing the edification of the body and building each other up?

Let's look at a few examples in scripture. In Acts 1 Jesus has already been crucified, and he's already resurrected. He has already ascended, but he has told them to wait in Jerusalem. They don't even know what they're waiting for, they're just waiting in an upper room.

But look what they did in Acts 1:12-16:

> Then they returned to Jerusalem from the Mount called Olivet, which is near Jerusalem, a Sabbath day's journey away. When they had entered the city, they went to the upper room where they were staying; that is Peter and John and James and Andrew, Philip and Thomas, Bartholomew and Matthew, James son of

> Alphaeus, and Simon the Zealot, and Judas the son of James. These all with one mind were continually devoting themselves to prayer, along with the women, and Mary the mother of Jesus, and with His brothers.

These, all with one mind, were continually devoting themselves to prayer. And then something happened and the people of Jerusalem said, "What is going on with you believers?" And Peter says, "what's going on right here is what you heard about in the book of Joel."

Acts 2:15 & 17:

> For these men are not drunk, as you suppose, for it's *only* the third hour of the day; but this is what was spoken of through the Prophet Joel: "And it shall be in the last days," God says, "That I will pour forth of My Spirit on all mankind; And your sons and your daughters shall prophesy."

Prophesy. What were they doing prior to the prophesying? They *were of one mind praying. They were in unity, in prayer*. They were literally saying, bring it Holy Spirit! What do you want for us, what do you have for us, how do you want to release this, and what do you want us to do? We're here together for you to do whatever you want to do, and to move however you want to move. We want to be released into whatever *You* have to give us.

We must also check our desires. What do we desire *right now* when it comes to the word of God?

1 Corinthians 14:39:

> Therefore, my brethren, *desire earnestly* to prophesy, and *do not forbid* to speak in tongues.

What evidence is there in your life that you want to speak from God to build someone else up?

This is what I believe actually happens, one of two things happens. One, I believe we are afraid, and we act out of fear when it comes to prophesy. I believe we're afraid that what we say may not have actually come from God, and that we were just making this up because we don't realize that we're actually hearing from the Holy Spirit. Thus, we're 'afraid to take the risk' and speak for God. One such person who attends my church on Wednesday evenings told me, "I'm really struggling with whether or not I'm hearing from the Holy Spirit. How can I tell if it's His voice or my voice? I'm trying to step into this by faith, but I don't always feel like I am." She was at church one Wednesday, but needed to leave for whatever reason, so she got in her car and left. She later told me, "I got right to the stop sign at the corner and something inside of me said, Go back, there's a word for you tonight." Now, I personally hadn't known where she went when she left the auditorium. I did not know she had left the building, I assumed she went to the restroom. But she came back in the room and the Lord gave me a word for her, so I spoke it to her. And she says, "I heard the Holy Spirit at the stop sign, and He told me to come back here! Then I come back in, and you have a word for me! With 200 people in the room, you had a word for me! It was amazing, and not only that, it confirmed the word *'He'* had just spoken to me!" So she has no more fear about whether or not she hears from God, God took that very moment of question for her, and confirmed exactly what she needed to hear, the very question she was asking Him, and He will do the same for you! The only way that we can know if we're hearing from the Spirit is to take the risk and act on it, we must take the risk to speak it out!

So many people don't prophesy because we're not sure we're hearing from *Him*, and the other reason we don't prophesy is also fear based–*we're afraid we're going to mess it up*!

Let's look at what we're forgetting. We forget we're a child of God, and that our Father knows how to train us up. Our Father knows how to protect our mistakes, our Father knows how to convict us, He'll tell us, "Don't say that. I didn't tell you to say that. Why are you saying that? Next time I give you something, just say what I tell you to say. Don't add to it." The beauty is, we'll be sitting in an auditorium, we'll look across the room and see somebody, and the

Spirit will say, impress on us, to "Go tell them that God loves them," and we will think, "Oh come on, that is so cliché. That had to have come from me. Can't you tell me something more specific, like maybe about their dog's cancer? You know, give me something really, really specific so I know I'm taking a risk." And Holy Spirit will say, "Are you going to do it or not?" So you muster the courage to go over and you say, "Look, I'm not real comfortable with this, I'm kind of new to it, but I feel like the Spirit told me to tell you that God loves you." Then you watch them break into tears. You watch them bend over and begin to bawl because you didn't know that they got up this morning and said, "God, I don't see you. I don't feel you. I feel far from you. I will go to church, but if I don't have some kind of encounter with you, I'm giving up." And that "God loves you" that you spoke to them in obedience, however awkward, was all they needed in that moment. Because of the fact that you heard from the Holy Spirit, took a risk and were obedient, they were edified and they were built up, and *their* faith was increased too!

Do you have a desire to be used by God to build someone else up? Do you desire to have a word that can be delivered? Paul says that we should have that as a desire, and yet here's what happens for most believers. Here's the mind game the enemy plays in our heads. Most believers have grown up in churches that don't understand this scripture or how to properly apply it. In fact, they actually teach that the gifts are not for today, that the gifts stopped or ceased with the apostles. How would this teaching and lack of understanding of scripture impact their ability to prophesy or take a risk to learn to prophesy? How can we take a risk if we're in a church that doesn't understand this scripture or even allow us to prophesy? How can we learn to exercise this gift if we've been made to feel shame, guilt or fear for even trying? How can we step out and be obedient when we are experiencing these negative emotions while trying to be faithful? If this is the case, then this scripture is for you. It may be that you need to be in an environment for awhile where you can learn this, receive this, and then practice. It can be difficult to receive a supernatural gift of the Spirit, such as prophesy, if you don't know or are not in an environment that supports this. As we see in Acts 19:1-6, the people in Ephesus had not even heard there was a Holy Spirit, they didn't know. But once they knew, then they could be baptized in the Holy Spirit and prophesy, and not only that, they could now receive ALL the supernatural gifts of the Holy Spirit!

> It happened that while Apollos was at Corinth, Paul passed through the upper country and came to Ephesus, and found some disciples. He said to them, “Did you receive the Holy Spirit when you believed?” And they said to him, “No, we haven't even heard whether there is a Holy Spirit.” And he said, “Into what then were you baptized?” And they said, “Into John's baptism.” Paul said, “John baptized with the baptism of repentance, telling the people to believe in Him who was coming after him, that is, in Jesus.” When they heard this, they were baptized in the name of the Lord Jesus. And when Paul had laid hands upon them, the Holy Spirit came on them, and they *began* speaking with tongues and prophesying.

It was not their fault they had not heard, but once they did and they learned about this new/different/other baptism, the baptism of the Holy Spirit, which is different from John’s baptism, and comes ‘after’ John’s baptism, *THEN* they began to speak in tongues *AND* prophesy! There has to be a communication channel within us! The spirit of man is dead because of sin, our spirits died in the garden when man sinned. But when we come to know Jesus Christ *and* believe in Him, it says our spirit is regenerated. We are born again, not in the flesh, *but in the spirit*! Our spirits are brought to life, then the Holy Spirit comes to dwell in our spirit, *and* we can receive the Baptism of the Holy Spirit! Now we have what we need, the Holy Spirit dwelling in us in order for us to communicate with God.

I believe this is a critical key that is missing in today’s church. The critical key and component is prophesying, speaking life into one another, encouraging one another, and building one another up. We should not be people who get together to compare our groans and moans and aches and pains. We should be the people who get together to compare our joys and our rejoicing and our praise and our prayers. God is good, and Paul is saying, you have a job in the church and your job in the church is to build others up *through* this gift of prophecy. We need to begin to sow words of prophecy, words of encouragement, words of edification, the very words of Christ into others.

Teaching 'should' prick our hearts when delivered in the Spirit, and prophecy should also prick the heart because it's a 'now' word from God. Let's see how differently the body of Christ looks when we start prophesying, when we speak words of edification and encouragement! We can be bold and speak and proclaim the word of the Lord!

HOLY SPIRIT IMPARTATION

A beautiful work of the Holy Spirit is impartation. To impart means to put something from someone or something into another. Biblically, to impart is a work of the Holy Spirit in giving spiritual gifts, such as through the baptism of the Holy Spirit for the work of the ministry. It is the transference of these gifts from one man or woman of God to another, through the Holy Spirit, especially by the laying on of hands. There are two very popular scriptures that are always used to teach on this.

The first scripture is Romans 1:11 where Paul says:

> For I long to see you so that I may impart some spiritual gift to you, that you may be established;

The other scripture is 2 Timothy 1:6:

> For this reason I remind you to kindle afresh the gift of God which is in you through the laying on of my hands.

These are probably the two most popular scriptures when it comes to the laying on of hands and impartation. Because of that, I'm not going to use either one in this teaching because I believe there are plenty more in scripture to support and to understand impartation, especially through the laying on of hands.

Let's go back and start in Hebrews 6:1:

> Therefore leaving the elementary teaching about the Christ, let us press on to maturity, not laying again a foundation of repentance from dead works and of faith

> toward God, of instruction about washings and laying on of hands, and the resurrection of the dead and eternal judgment.

The scripture says that we are going to go beyond the elementary teachings. Let us press on to maturity, let's be done with the simple teaching, and let's move on to the more mature teachings. Then he gives us a list of what the simple teachings are: repentance from dead works, faith toward God, instructions about washings, laying on of hands, the resurrection of the dead and eternal judgment.

Those are the simple things, resurrection from the dead, a simple thing. Eternal judgment is a simple thing. What has happened is, he has already talked about repentance. Peter said from the very beginning, repent each one of you. Jesus says to repent for the Kingdom of God is at hand. He has also talked about faith; there is conviction in the belief of Jesus, his death and resurrection, and its application for you. Hebrews 11:6 says it's impossible to please God without faith. He also spoke of washings. We should notice it said washings, plural. If we go back into the Greek, the word for washings used here is "baptisma;" does that sound familiar? Paul is talking about the baptisms because he started with what they knew, which was the laver washing at the temple with water. Now he says, there are washings, there's a baptism into Christ. There's a water baptism, and there's a baptism in the Spirit. Then he goes on to say the laying on of hands, which is what we'll talk about in this chapter. Paul also spoke of the resurrection of the dead; in 1 Corinthians 15, there's an entire conversation about the resurrection of the dead. Next, eternal judgment; we can see how that plays out in Revelation 20. But he says these are fundamental things, these are simple concepts. And one of them is the laying on of hands, impartation through the laying on of the hands.

What I want to start with is looking biblically at the history of laying on of hands. Where did it start that we would be using it today in the New Covenant? We can go back to the Old Covenant and begin to see how it was used then. We need to remember that *everything in the Old Covenant is a physical representation of a spiritual concept in the New Covenant.* We can go back to the Old Testament to see how what happened in the physical helps us understand the spiritual concept today.

If we go back to Leviticus, in chapters 4 and 8 there was a sacrificial system put in place. In this process, a man could be redeemed and atone for his sin before Jesus Christ came. This worked by taking a one-year-old unblemished lamb in which the priest would go and lay hands on the lamb. When he laid hands on that lamb, he would transfer the sin of man to the lamb and then they would sacrifice the lamb. The blood of that lamb would be sprinkled on the Ark of the Covenant, and thru the sacrifice and the blood, the atonement for sin would be given to man. Needless to say, Jesus has been that lamb for us, so there is a transfer, if you will, in the spiritual realm of our sins of man onto the lamb of God, Jesus.

If we move forward into Numbers chapter 27, Moses lays hands on Joshua to commission him, but he actually transfers something to Joshua in Numbers 27:18:

> So the Lord said to Moses, "Take Joshua the son of Nun, a man in whom is the Spirit, and lay your hand on him; and have him stand before Eleazar the priest and before all the congregation, and commission him in their sight. You shall put some of your authority on him, in order that all the congregation of the sons of Israel may obey *him*.

God said, take Joshua and put him in front of the people and put your hands on him so that some of your authority can be transferred upon him. Therefore, the people will follow him. There was a transfer of Moses's authority, an impartation to Joshua of authority from Moses.

In Genesis chapter 48, Israel (previously Jacob) is praying over his grandsons, Ephraim and Manasseh, and in 48:14 it says:

> But Israel stretched out his right hand and laid it on the head of Ephraim, who was the younger, and his left hand on Manasseh's head, crossing his hands, although

> Manasseh was the firstborn. He blessed Joseph and said, "The God before whom my fathers Abraham and Isaac walked, The God who has been my shepherd all my life to this day, The Angel who has redeemed me from all evil, Bless the lads; And may my name live on in them, And the names of my fathers Abraham and Isaac; And may they grow into a multitude in the midst of the earth."

Israel passed on the blessing that was from Abraham and Isaac onto his grandsons. He also said, may I live on through them. There is a blessing that got transferred.

We see that there is a transfer of something that occurs through the laying on of hands. That's why God instructs them to put their hands *on* the person. Initially, hands were laid on animals so that sins could be transferred to the animal. On another occasion, authority was transferred, for instance, Moses laid his hands on Joshua to transfer authority. Other times it is a blessing that is transferred as Israel laid hands on his grandsons to pass on a blessing.

So we see there is a transfer of something spiritual, we physically lay hands on someone, but what is happening is spiritual. It's not covering our hands in something to put a physical mark, it's the laying on of hands and speaking a blessing or authority. If there's no transfer going on in the spiritual realm, then why would we lay hands on someone? *Impartation is the transfer of something in the spiritual realm from one to another.* But a lot of people, a lot of believers actually, struggle with impartation. I believe there has been a lot of abuse as it concerns impartation, so a lot of people struggle with the laying on of hands. But in reality, it is straight up biblical from the very beginning. From the beginning of our walk with God, he says lay your hands on them and transfer. We can't discard biblical things because some have abused them through the years.

Now, let's look at the New Testament biblical occurrences of laying on of hands, what was the purpose of laying on of hands in the New Testament, and was it for the same or different reasons as in the Old Testament?

In 1 Timothy 4:14 Paul says to Timothy:

> Do not neglect the spiritual gift within you, which was bestowed on you through prophetic utterance with the laying on of hands by the presbytery.

What did Paul just say? He said there's a gift in you that you received because we spoke it and laid hands on you. When we spoke and laid hands on you, the gift was transferred to you, and it was a spiritual thing, it was a gift imparted to you by the laying on of hands.

In other words, impartation, the imparting of something from one to another, can come through the mouth, through the word itself, with the laying on of hands. What is it that can be imparted to someone else through words in the laying on of our hands? We've already seen that authority and blessing can be passed on and imparted, but let's continue to examine the New Covenant for additional impartations.

Mark 6:5 says this about Jesus:

> And He could do no miracle there except that He laid His hands on a few sick people and healed them.

And in Acts 9:17:

> So Ananias departed and entered the house, and after laying his hands on him said, "Brother Saul, the Lord Jesus, who appeared to you on the road by which you were coming, has sent me so that you may regain your sight and be filled with the Holy Spirit."

Acts 28:8:

> And it happened that the father of Publius was lying in bed afflicted with recurrent fever and dysentery; and Paul went in to see him and after he had prayed, he laid his hands on him and healed him.

These are examples of where there was an impartation of healing that came through the laying on of hands.

So, the question is, does this still work today, and does God work through us in this way?

Let's look in Mark 16:15-18:

> And He said to them, "Go into all the world and preach the gospel to all creation. He who has believed and has been baptized shall be saved; but he who has disbelieved shall be condemned. These signs will accompany those who have believed: in My name they will cast out demons, they will speak with new tongues; they will pick up serpents, and if they drink any deadly *poison*, it will not hurt them; they will lay hands on the sick, and they will recover."

This is the sign of a believer. JESUS said these signs will follow the believer, that they will lay hands on people and they will recover from their sickness. It is a spiritual act of miraculous healing that takes place through the impartation, through the laying on of hands; it is a spiritual thing being done through the hands. This is God's system, not our system, we didn't come up with this, God came up with this. Why didn't God tell us to just speak to someone rather than lay hands on them *AND* speak? Why does He say we need to lay hands on them too? We don't have the answer to that; we'll need to ask Him.

There is also the commissioning of people for service in Acts 6:3-6:

> "Therefore, brethren, select from among you seven men of good reputation, full of the Spirit and of wisdom, whom we may put in charge of this task. But we will devote ourselves to prayer and to the ministry of the word." The statement found approval with the whole congregation; and they chose Stephen, a man full of faith and of the Holy Spirit, and Philip, Prochorus, Nicanor, Timon, Parmenas and Nicolas, a

> proselyte from Antioch. And these they brought before the apostles; and after praying, they laid their hands on them.

There is a group of people complaining that they weren't getting fed in the daily feeding. The Apostles basically said, look, we don't have time to get involved in this; we need to be praying and spending our time in the word, so let's find somebody who can handle this task; and they chose these seven men. They commissioned them into the work. They imparted to them the ability to serve in this kind of leading role by laying hands on them.

Another thing we see regarding impartation is in Acts 8 and Acts 19. It shows us here that helping someone to be baptized in the Spirit comes through the laying on of hands.

In Acts 8:14-17:

> Now when the apostles in Jerusalem heard that Samaria had received the word of God, they sent them Peter and John, who came down and prayed for them that they might receive the Holy Spirit. For He had not yet fallen upon any of them; they had simply been baptized in the name of the Lord Jesus. Then they *began* laying their hands on them, and they were receiving the Holy Spirit.

I don't want this to be a confusion to you if you're new to understanding how this works. When you come to know Christ, when you put your faith in Christ, you are sealed and indwelled by the Holy Spirit. Ephesians 1:13 says this:

> In Him, you also, after listening to the message of truth, the gospel of your salvation—having also believed, you were sealed in Him with the Holy Spirit of promise, who is given as a pledge of our inheritance, with a view to the redemption of *God's own* possession, to the praise of His glory.

So we're sealed with the Spirit. But on the day of Pentecost, Jesus told His followers, His disciples, to go to Jerusalem after he had given them the Spirit as recorded in John 20:22. And He said, "*now wait* until the Spirit comes upon you with power." (Acts 1:5 & 8) And we notice here that it says he had not come upon them yet. So, there was a baptism in the Spirit that they hadn't received yet. They were sealed. They were indwelled, but there was a power that needed to come upon them that hadn't been released. And it was released to them by impartation thru the laying on of hands.

Another example is In Acts 19:1-6:

> It happened that while Apollos was at Corinth, Paul passed through the upper country and came to Ephesus, and found some disciples. He said to them, "Did you receive the Holy Spirit when you believed?" And they *said* to him, "No, we have not even heard whether there is a Holy Spirit." And he said, "Into what then were you baptized?" And they said, "Into John's baptism." Paul said, "John baptized with the baptism of repentance, telling the people to believe in Him who was coming after him, that is, in Jesus." When they heard this, they were baptized in the name of the Lord Jesus. And when Paul had laid his hands upon them, the Holy Spirit came on them, and they *began* speaking with tongues and prophesying.

We see here that our role in assisting with the baptism of the Holy Spirit can be through the laying on of hands.

So why is the laying on of hands sometimes a controversial topic in churches? Why do we shy away from TV programs and churches where we see this happening? I want to go ahead and address the elephant in the room right now, because I believe the elephant in the room for those who may be new to the things of the Spirit is actually this issue. Sometimes there can be abuses of this, but I think more often than not, it's misunderstanding. What is happening when sometimes hands are laid on someone and they fall down? What is that about? How does that work in this impartation of the laying on of the hands, and what is happening? What is this 'falling down thing' that is often called "falling out in the Spirit."

First, we must recognize from what we've just learned, if there is a transfer in the spiritual realm, then *something* is going on *in the spirit* when we lay hands on someone. What we get a little nervous about is how does that transfer manifest? Let me show you what I mean. If we laid hands on someone and we begin to pray over them and they begin to cry, nobody has a problem. "Oh Wow. It must be something really special going on there" is what we say. If we lay hands on somebody and they bow down and begin to weep, we might say, "Man, they're having a moment, aren't they?" If we lay hands on them and they fall to their knees and they begin to pray, we believe an intense work of God is going on, right? Sometimes we lay hands on people, and they raise their hands and everybody's okay with that. We believe, this person's "in the moment" and they're receiving, it's a *good* thing. But if we lay hands on them and they start shaking, eyebrows raise. What's this about? Or if we lay hands on them and they fall over backwards, then we get into this conversation of, is that real? Is that biblical? Could that possibly be happening? Is that true?

Let's look at John 18:4-6, which says:

> So Jesus, knowing all the things that were coming upon Him, went forth and said to them, "Whom do you seek?" They answered Him, "Jesus the Nazarene." He said to them, "I am *He*." And Judas also, who was betraying Him, was standing with them. So when He said to them, "I am *He*," they drew back and fell to the ground.

And I've had person after person say, "Yeah, but that's Jesus. That's for Jesus only. When Jesus says, I am He, yeah, of course they would fall back on the ground." And yet we profess to believe the scripture that says; Christ lives in me (Gal 2:20). How can this scripture be true for some things, and not for others?

What we need to do is watch ourselves so that we don't make a rule book out of the Bible. It's so easy to decide that certain things are good and certain things are bad, and the things we don't understand go immediately into the bad category. What happens is that we don't learn the character of God through scripture, and we try to make the scripture a rulebook of God. If you don't believe this, Jesus addressed it. Jesus actually addressed that very topic in Matthew 23. Listen to what he's explaining, and let's see if we can get the *concept* of what he's saying.

Matthew 23:16-22:

> "Woe to you, blind guides, who say, 'Whoever swears by the temple, that is nothing; but whoever swears by the gold of the temple is obligated.' You fools and blind men! Which is more important, the gold or the temple that sanctified the gold? And, 'Whoever swears by the altar, *that* is nothing, but whoever swears by the offering on it, he is obligated.' You blind men, which is more important, the offering, or the altar that sanctifies the offering? Therefore, whoever swears by the altar, swears both by the altar and by everything on it. And whoever swears by the temple, swears *both* by the temple and by Him who dwells within it. And whoever swears by heaven, swears *both* by the throne of God and by Him who sits upon it.

What did Jesus just say? Stop making everything into rules. You say the offering is most important, then you swear by the altar, and it doesn't matter. The offering is not an offering unless it's put *on* the altar.

So sometimes *WE* create rules '*for God*', about what He can and cannot do. It gets crazy because what God is saying is, why are you dissecting this? Either I'm here or I'm not. Look in the Spirit, determine and access spiritually, look at My character, and use *your spirit* to discern and determine what's going on.

Is there flesh in the laying on of hands? Sometimes. Just as there is flesh in many aspects of the body and the church. What do we call it when people look around the room judging others, while ignoring their own sin. That’s also flesh, so will there be people who “courtesy fall.” Yes, but don't miss the point. What God is saying is, there's something I'm doing, and you're breaking it down into a rule, and you're missing the point. Let’s look at a really important scripture for this.

John 21:25 says:

> And there are also many other things which Jesus did, which if they were written in detail, I suppose that even the world itself would not contain the books that would be written.

What John says is, Jesus did so many things we didn't even tell you about! *We wouldn't even be able to record all that he did!* If we draw a hard line that nothing is legitimate unless we’ve already seen it in scripture, then what we're saying is that all of these other things were just Jesus repeating what is already recorded, and all of these other things had to be identical to what was written down.

If we take this stance, then we're fully missing the character of God!

We're fully missing the character of Jesus in trying to conform scripture into our own personal comfort boxes. I'm not being mean about it, but I am saying yes, there is flesh sometimes, but we can’t neglect the things of God because we don't understand it all yet, and *we CANNOT overlook the character of God*. He is the same God. The same God who gives an impartation that would cause someone to fall out also put Peter in a trance in Acts 11. Jesus breathes on people to deliver the Holy Spirit in John 20. A Priest can't stand in the glory of the Lord in 1 Kings 8. Through an angel, God shuts Zachariah's mouth, and for months he can't speak, Luke 1. Jesus, stating that He was Jesus, made the guards fall out. Ezekiel, *and this is a crazy story*, Ezekiel spends 390 days lying on the ground on his left-hand side, and after that he gets up and lies 40 days on his right-hand side. Over 400 days Ezekiel is laying on the ground because God has said, I need you to do this for Judah and for Israel. My question is, what is in the character of God?

The way to truly assess these things is to look for fruit. What was the difference because someone fell out in the Spirit? Ask that person, they can tell you what happened. "This is who I am now, this is just what got changed, this is my new identity, this is what the Lord spoke to me." Look for the fruit. Instead of us telling God what he can and cannot do during a time of impartation, we should be looking for the evidence of the impartation. That is the best measure of the credibility of the process.

The laying on of hands is a serious issue in scripture, so serious that it comes with a warning. In 1 Timothy, they're talking about appointing elders and understanding the role of an elder and in 1 Timothy 5:22 it says:

> Do not lay hands upon anyone *too* hastily and thereby share responsibility for the sins of others; keep yourself free from sin.

What is Paul saying? If we're going to move somebody into the role of Elder, we better know their character! We better know their spirit, we need to discern that there won't be something that will cause problems later because their character and their spirit is not right.

Lets delve deeper biblically to see more examples of the impartation. We have examples in Genesis 48 of the transfer of a blessing through the laying on of hands, and another example of the commissioning of someone to impart authority is in Numbers 27. Laying on of hands when sending out leaders is seen in Acts 13. (We can see more examples in the chapter titled, Holy Spirit Direction). We see the laying on of hands in the recognizing of church servants in Acts 6, and we see it to aid in the receiving of the baptism and the Holy Spirit in Acts 8 and 19. Also in the recovery of the sick in Mark 6, and in the impartation of a gift in Deuteronomy 34 when Moses imparts a gift of wisdom to Joshua and in 1 Timothy. We also read that we can impart with our words through prophecy and through teaching in 1 Corinthians 12 through 14. What do we learn from this list? We learn that there is a thing in the Kingdom of God called impartation. It is necessary because something is *IN US* that needs to be passed on and given to someone else.

Do you remember in Acts 3 that Peter and John are going into the temple, and there's a man that is lame? He was asking for money, but don't miss the point. Peter said, I don't possess silver and gold, but what I do have, in the name of Jesus Christ the Nazarene, walk. The scripture says he grabbed him by the hand and he pulled him up to walk. That's interesting, it's interesting that he didn't say rise up and walk and then stand there and watch. But he actually reached out with his hand and pulled the man to his feet. You may say that he was just helping him up, but there are other examples in scripture where no help was offered. I believe there was an impartation of healing in this act.

What does this matter for you and me? What would it mean for us in the Christian walk? I believe there are things of the Kingdom of God in many of us that need to be imparted. They have been locked up in us because we don't understand impartation. What do I mean by that? What if we had the opportunity to lay hands on somebody and they got healed? Would we do it? Yes. There is a spiritual impartation of healing, and that's what it is. These gifts are in us, in all believers, waiting to be released, and we are holding them unreleased because of our lack of knowledge, lack of learning, lack of practice and sometimes even lack of faith. If the same Spirit that raised Jesus from the dead lives inside of us, then why do we limit what that Spirit could do in us?

I'm over 50, so I know some may not be familiar with this, but years ago there used to be a novelty device that was a small ring that went around one's finger, and it had a buzzer that was positioned in the palm of the hand so that when one shook hands with someone, it actually gave them a 'shock'. Impartation operates in a similar way, in that when something is imparted, it may seem like a jolt or even a buzz. Sitting in my office thinking of this, I asked God about it, I said, "you know, this is such a broad topic. There is so much going on with this, and there is so much information, and I don't want it to just be information or more head knowledge. I don't want this to come across as informational, but motivational! I want it to be something we learn about so that we can do, this needs to be more than just information, it must also be action! So Holy Spirit, what do you want me to do?" And he said, "remember the hand buzzer?"

And the thought came to me that I could teach all about impartation, and at the very end I could say, remember to go out with your hand buzzer because there's power in you that needs to be imparted to someone else! What a great analogy and reminder!

How would we demonstrate the power of the Holy Spirit if all we had was medical medicine? Medical doctors are great, and they are amazing, so we don't need to reject medical help. But there are people who say, "Well, I'm not going to go to a doctor, I will trust in the Holy Spirit to heal me." There is common sense, and if I were to break a glass in my sink and cut my hand open, I'm not going to stand there and say, "Come together and be healed, skin!" I'm going to go get that thing stitched up. That's not a lack of faith, it's, I don't want to bleed to death while I'm standing here using my faith.

I am also not making light of healing, and this is what I am saying. There is something put in us by the Holy Spirit, and it wasn't put there by the Spirit so we could hold it in a jar or keep it to ourselves. It was put in us so that it can ALSO be poured out on others, it was put there by the Spirit so that we could pass it on, it was put there by the Spirit for the common good of the church. Someone in authority could lay hands on people who need authority to do what they're called to do in the body. Someone who works in healing could lay hands on people who are about to go somewhere where people need healing. They need that impartation to heal. If there's someone in a church who works in teaching and wisdom and knowledge, they can lay hands on someone who is called to teach, who doesn't want to do it without wisdom and knowledge. There's an impartation that is part of our history as believers that goes all the way back to the fathers of our faith, so we have to recognize that the Holy Spirit wants to do work in someone else, 'through us,' and He is waiting for us to release the Holy Spirit to them.

I cannot think of a greater honor than to be used by the very Spirit of God to release His power into someone else's life. You may be thinking, "Man, I don't know where this goes. I don't understand this Spirit, power, laying hands, and releasing thing, I'm not even sure I understand the Holy Spirit or this extra baptism and power that you're talking about. I don't understand how He dwells in me, and I don't even know how I would receive the Holy Spirit's power in me, much less impart it."

Listen, God created us, He created a world and a people, and He put them on this earth just for the purpose of loving them. Then He gave them all rights and authority over the earth, and He put a tree in the garden and said, don't eat from this tree. Why? Because we had to have a choice to love Him, the tree was the choice to love and follow God. It's not love if we're forced, but if we have a choice, we can choose to love God. So God creates man, and puts him in the garden. But then satan comes into the garden and tells the man, whom God created, "You know what, nothing bad is going to happen to you if you eat from that tree. What will actually happen, is you will become more like God, knowing good from evil, wouldn't that be cool!" And man, instead of following the instruction of God, follows the instruction of satan. In other words, man submits to whomever he is listening to and taking directions from, and instead of listening to God and following His instruction, they're now submitting to satan, and it causes a divide between man and God. But God loves us so much that He steps in instantly and says, "I will fix this. I will fix this because one day I'm going to send my son as a man to this earth, and he's going to walk out life just like you. He will be tempted in every way that you're tempted, yet He will do it without sinning, without breaking the relationship between Me and Him."

Why in the world is that important? It had to happen that way because Jesus has a righteous standing with God. He's never done anything to break His relationship with God, and He's never done anything against God. But the Bible says that all of us, every one of us, you and I, all of us have sinned and fallen short of God's glory. We've broken our relationship with God, but there was one, and only one, named Jesus who never sinned. So how does that help us? He took all of the punishment that was due to you and to me, for the way that we dishonored, disobeyed, and disrespected God. He took it all on Himself at the cross.

He was brutally beaten, whipped, mocked, and a crown of thorns was placed on His head. He was crucified, *taking all of the punishment for all of man's sin*. Why? Why would He do that? He did it because he was righteous with God, because there was nothing about Him that would create any separation from God, and we had something in us that created a separation from God, and that's our sin. We were due a separation from God, a condemnation. We didn't follow him, we didn't submit to him. Every one of us has sinned and is therefore separated from God. The Bible says that each one has gone his own way, but the iniquity has been laid on Him. What Jesus said and has done for us is, He said, "I'll take your punishment, and if you'll believe in what I did for you, then you can have my righteousness."

You see Jesus, who knew no sin, became sin 'for us' so that we might become in right standing with God in Christ. What does that mean? It means he took all of our condemnation on the cross, all of our punishment for everything we've ever done against God, and that one day we are going to stand before God. Most people are going to try to convince God that they were good people. "I read the Bible, I went to church. I prayed at every meal. I'm a good person. Ask anybody, I'm a good person." Let me ask you this, "What separated Adam and Eve from God?" Just one disobedience, don't eat from the tree, and they did. That's why we are all guilty, it only took one sin to make us guilty. But the beauty of the story is Jesus is *NOT* guilty, and He says in His 'not guilty' state, that He will take all of our punishment for us 'so that' there is no punishment due us. So when we stand before God, instead of trying to convince God that we're a good person, we'll stand before God and say, "I was unrighteous. But there's nothing to punish me for. You've already punished Jesus in my place. You poured out your wrath on Him, not me. I stand before you, hidden in Christ."

This is the beauty of the Gospel. The good news of Jesus Christ is that for everyone who believes, for everyone who believes they need to be reconciled with God, for everyone who believes that they've sinned, and everyone who knows their relationship with God is busted, for any of us, if we believe that what Jesus did was done for us, we can be saved. Jesus took the punishment and says, will you believe it so it can be applied to you, because if you believe that He did it for you, then He did it for you.

When you stand before God, what have you got to present? Your goodness, your kindness, the fact that you are a nice person or that you went to church? The question will be, did you sin… at all… ever?

But, what you can present is Jesus. Jesus took all the punishment for you so that you can be righteous before God. Would you be willing to believe that today, right now, in this moment? Would you be willing to say to God, I know my relationship with you is broken. I have done things you told me not to do. I've not done the things you've told me to do, but I want to fix that today through Jesus. I believe that Jesus Christ was punished on a cross to his death for my sin, and I believe through the power of the Holy Spirit, that He was raised from the dead to show me there's a life after this one and that he could give me eternal life with you, God. I believe that He did that for me, and when I stand before you God, I will say I'm hidden in Christ. I believe that He did that for me, and I put my faith in what he did on the cross for my life.

Today, if you're willing to say that, just say it to God, and He will hear you. Say to God, forgive me, I'm going to repent, and I'm asking you to send your Holy Spirit because when your Spirit comes, I'm not by myself in this. I'm not by myself in changing my ways. The Spirit gives me new desires. The Spirit shows me and teaches me and trains me. I can walk in your ways because I will be equipped with something I didn't have before, the Holy Spirit. Today, I believe and accept what Jesus did for me on the cross. Thank you God for forgiving me and saving me.

HOLY SPIRIT DIRECTION

I believe direction is something most believers are looking for, and I think it's something we all want. We want direction from God, and we want to be led by the Holy Spirit. I believe many of us have been waiting for that direction, waiting for that next thing, waiting to hear from the Lord, wanting to know: What is my plan? What is my purpose? What am I going to? Is there a ministry? Is there a greater call on my life? And I think for many people, there's a frustration that grows. It's a frustration that grows because of our desire to receive a call and to be used in The Kingdom. We wonder what is going on if we haven't seen something big come to fruition yet.

We say things like: Why am I not moving forward in my calling if I'm available?

So let's look at the process of the call in four distinct points laid out in Acts 13:1-12:

> Now there were at Antioch, in the church that was *there*, prophets and teachers: Barnabas, and Simeon who was called Niger, and Lucius of Cyrene, and Manaen who had been brought up with Herod the tetrarch, and Saul. While they were ministering to the Lord and fasting, the Holy Spirit said, "Set apart for Me Barnabas and Saul for the work to which I have called them." Then, when they had fasted and prayed and laid their hands on them, they sent them away.
>
> So, being sent out by the Holy Spirit, they went down to Seleucia and from there they sailed to Cyprus. When they reached Salamis, they *began* to proclaim the word of God in the synagogues of the Jews; and they also

> had John as their helper. When they had gone through the whole island as far as Paphos, they found a magician, a Jewish false prophet whose name was Bar-Jesus, who was with the proconsul, Sergius Paulus, a man of intelligence. This man summoned Barnabas and Saul and sought to hear the word of God. But Elymas the magician (for so his name is translated) was opposing them, seeking to turn the proconsul away from the faith. But Saul, who was also *known as* Paul, filled with the Holy Spirit, fixed his gaze on him, and said, "You who are full of all deceit and fraud, you son of the devil, you enemy of all righteousness, will you not cease to make crooked the straight ways of the Lord? Now, behold, the hand of the Lord is upon you, and you will be blind and not see the sun for a time." And immediately a mist and a darkness fell upon him, and he went about seeking those who would lead him by the hand. Then the proconsul believed when he saw what had happened, being amazed at the teaching of the Lord.

There's a lot in this scripture. There's a lot about how the Holy Spirit "sets us apart," how He "calls us," "sends us out" and "fills us." So let's start where it says the Holy Spirit said to them, "set apart for me Barnabas and Saul for the work to which I have called them." Set them apart. They are unique in this call. They are different from the others. They are identified as unique. I think God is dividing up Kingdom people for Kingdom purpose and setting them apart for this unique purpose. We know that when we go back and look in the book of Leviticus, God says we are a nation set apart.

In Leviticus 20:24-26:

Hence, I have said to you, "You are to possess their land, and I Myself will give it to you to possess it, a land flowing with milk and honey." I am the Lord your God, who has separated you from the peoples. You are therefore to make a distinction between the clean animal and the unclean, and between the unclean bird and the clean; and

> you shall not make yourselves detestable by animal or by bird or by anything that creeps on the ground, which I have separated for you as unclean. Thus you are to be holy to Me, for I the Lord am holy; and I have set you apart from the peoples to be Mine.

So we know at this time God is saying I am setting you apart as my people, and one of the ways you will be set apart is that you will not eat things that I designate as unclean. You'll become detestable if you engage in eating these things that I call unclean. We know that as we go through the Law and look at all of the physical do's and don'ts, we see, don't do this, but do these things. These rules are what they were under in the process of coming to know Him.

But we are no longer under this covenant, we're under a New Covenant, and we know that the Old Covenant is a physical representation of spiritual concepts that we grab ahold of today in the New Covenant. So, what is God saying to us today? What would we do that would make us unclean? Is there something we would eat that would make us unclean, or is it something else?

I'm looking at Matthew 15:10-11, and this is what it says:

> After Jesus called the crowd to Him, He said to them, "Hear and understand. It is not what enters into the mouth that defiles the man, but what proceeds out of the mouth, this defiles the man."

So now it's not what goes into a man, but what comes out? Why is he making that point under the New Covenant? I think it's because three chapters earlier in Matthew 12:33-34 he said this:

> Either make the tree good and its fruit good or make the tree bad and its fruit bad; for the tree is known by its fruit. You brood of vipers, how can you, being evil, speak what is good? For the mouth speaks out of that which fills the heart.

He goes on to say it's not what you take in that defiles you. It's what you speak out because what you speak out is what you are full of in your heart. So in the role of being "set apart" as a believer, it's not about rules to follow. It's also not about the food we eat. The role of being "set apart" as a believer is about our hearts. When the heart is right, obedience is no problem. When the heart is right, we don't need external controls. And for our heart to be right, what we need is internal transformation! When the heart is transformed, then what is spoken from the heart is life! What is spoken from a transformed heart does not defile a man.

The scripture goes on to say the Holy Spirit said, "set apart for me Barnabas and Saul for the work to which I have called them." So we talked about being "set apart" and the importance of the heart in being set apart. Now he says they're "called," and in order to be called, we must first be set apart. In order to be called, we have to be trusted; and in order to be trusted, we have to have a track record with God. If we have a track record with God, it shows we can be trusted, and the Holy Spirit can call us into ministry. I want to look at something in that same sentence which is really important. He said Barnabas and Saul were set apart to be called to a work. They are being called to a work. For any who might believe ministry is fluff, roses and benefits, He's saying that it's not–it's work! If we are looking for fluff and benefits, a secular job might be easier. Too many times, people want to be in ministry for a position, a title, respect, and maybe even fame. The reality is that titles do not define us, character does. Being in ministry is work and it's about leading the people of God.

Often people don't respect leaders because they don't like to follow, and sometimes it's because they have not been leaders themselves. It's easier to follow a leader if you have been a leader because you know how challenging it is. If the expectation is popularity, and it does not come, if you can't meet the expectations of the masses, and you wonder what am I doing here, discouragement can set in. I believe there's a reason why the Holy Spirit says there is a "work" that I called you to. I worked in manufacturing for 20 years with as many as five hundred people reporting to me. Do you know what they did? Whatever I asked. Why, because they were paid to. They did the work that was asked, without question, and the system worked well. In secular work, people do their work to keep their income. Hopefully they love their jobs and their work too! However, in ministry, when working with 500 volunteers, it's a totally different ballgame. I won't even get into what all that can mean. But the point is, being called into ministry is a call into the work of The Kingdom, whether it's paid or as a volunteer. All of our work should be done earnestly, as unto the Lord, as any work that we do should be.

Now lets look at the second point. The Holy Spirit called out two major players from the pack. You may not know this, but Barnabas was in Antioch, and Saul was in Tarsus. In Acts 11 it says Barnabas left Antioch to go to Tarsus to find Paul and verse 26 says:

> And when he found him, he brought him to Antioch. And for an entire year they met with the church and taught considerable numbers; and the disciples were first called Christians in Antioch.

What am I saying? Paul and Barnabas were a couple of major players in Antioch, whom the Holy Spirit was calling out of the pack. They had been there for a year. They invested their time, they taught, and they had paid their dues BEFORE they were called and sent out! Many people come to our church, Revive Church in Stuart Florida, and they may be new and have a leadership gift. They have great potential and have already been working in a ministry. Do you know what we ask them? We ask them to be with us for at least six months before seeking ministry or a leadership position, and there is a reason for this. Is it so we can get to know them? Important as that it, it's actually so they can get to know us. So they can understand the call of God on this church and see if He's calling them to be a part of this vision and calling. They must be called by God to be part of the vision here before they can become part of the leadership or service here, and this takes time. Sometimes people come desiring leadership before they even know who we are or what our calling is, and sometimes they desire to lead before serving. It is a process that takes time: align with the vision, serve, then lead.

Oftentimes we may be called out of the local church body because God may have a place of service somewhere else in The Kingdom. The Holy Spirit may pull us out of a local church to have us serve somewhere else in The Kingdom. Just know that when He calls you, it won't be a surprise.

Most of us know Romans 8:28 well:

> And we know that God causes all things to work together for good to those who love God, to those who are called according to *His* purpose. For those whom He foreknew, He also predestined to become conformed to the image of His Son, so that He would be the firstborn among many brethren; and these whom He predestined, He also called; and these whom He called, He also justified; and these whom He justified, He also glorified.

I gave this demonstration in church one day. I called a man out of the audience and I said: "Mike, come up here please. Can you stand right here, Mike." Then I asked the congregation, "Why did Mike come up here?" They answered, because I called him to come up here. That's why Mike was standing up at the front. When I called Mike to the front, I foreknew that I was going to call him up there even though he did not know that I was going to call him. As a matter of fact, he was sitting there studying something in his Bible when I called him. There was a pre-determined reason on my part to call him up front. He was predestined to be right up front because my decision was to call him there. He had no purpose to come up there until I called him. Truth be known, if he had come up there when I did not call him, I would have said, "Mike, go sit down please." And do you know what else? If Mike came up here on his own and milled around waiting for me to do something with him, I would have said, "Mike, you're just being a distraction, now please go sit down."

What was my point in that demonstration? This may be difficult to hear, so I'll explain in more detail what I mean.

Our availability does not create our call!

Our study of scripture, our knowledge, and even our experience does not create our call. Our desire to be called does not create our call, and our request to be used does not create our call. The only one who creates our call is God through His Holy Spirit; He decides when, where, why, and how to call us. There is no calling for us until He decides to call us!

I know this can be helpful for some to hear. I know that many believers are waiting and wanting that call, but I want to caution of the mistake we can make. We can force ourselves into a position or into a call that the Holy Spirit did not call us into. We can show up at the wrong place at the wrong time. We know in advance that we're called, because we're all actually called. We don't have to help the Holy Spirit by walking through every open door. We don't need to assume because there's a need to fill, that it's for us. It might be for someone else who isn't available or answering their call yet. There's nothing wrong with serving until we receive the call. The caution is to not open doors that are not yet open, that are not meant for us, or are not yet in the proper time. As long as we're not prematurely pushing ourselves through, we're ok. The fact is, we're miserable if we push things through in the flesh, because we're not in alignment with God and the call of the Holy Spirit for that call or position. The Spirit decides when to call us; we don't decide when, where or how we're called.

You might ask, "well, what do I do until he calls, what do I do until then?" Obedience is from the heart. Just make sure that what's coming from the fullness of your heart doesn't defile you. Make sure that you're speaking the truth in love, and if you're not called yet, since you will be called to work, just be grateful for where you are right now. Be grateful that you have some time before you're called, because when he calls, I promise it will be work!

The next thing it says is that they were "sent out" by the Holy Spirit. The Spirit sets the direction in which we are to be sent out, and this is huge. Sometimes the call to be sent is not necessarily a physical move. It's easy to get comfortable where we are; we like the familiar; we want be used where we are now. We know how it works; we know the people and the environment. It's comfortable to us. Sometimes God might do something totally unexpected that flips everything around.

Sometimes He lets us stay where we are and still be sent out. What do I mean by this? We can be sent out of our "traditional ways." We can be sent out of our "religious views." We can be sent out of our timidity. We can be sent out of a secular job, or we can be sent out of the country, which I think is what people fear most. The fear for many is, what if God calls me to some foreign country or out of my comfort zone? What if I have to live in a hut in some remote village; we don't know if we can handle that.

There's a scripture that says, God gives us the desires of our heart, and this is important to hear. This has nothing to do with us. That's right, it has nothing to do with us. He is not doing what we want. In this scripture, God is saying, I will give you the desires… of your heart. The desire that is there is the desire given to us by God. The desires we have actually come from Him. God gives us desires. God will give us a desire to live in a mud hut so that when He calls us, there's an alignment in our heart. God will give us the desires that He needs us to have so that when He calls us, we're in alignment with what He calls us to. So let's look at Luke 10:1-3:

> Now after this the Lord appointed seventy others, and sent them in pairs ahead of Him to every city and place where He Himself was going to come. And He was saying to them, 'The harvest is plentiful, but the laborers are few; therefore, beseech the Lord of the harvest to send out laborers into His harvest. Go; behold, I send you out as lambs in the midst of wolves.'

This is important to note: If the Holy Spirit calls us to something, it is impossible for us to go without the Holy Spirit, because the Holy Spirit lives in us. If the Holy Spirit calls us to a place, it is because God wants the Holy Spirit's presence in that place. So wherever we are going is where He is going because we are taking Him with us to that place. Does that make sense? Sometimes we're being called, not because we're so great, but because the Spirit wants to be in a place, at a time, for a purpose, and he's going to use us to go. This is why we're "set apart;" this is why we're "called"–it's so much bigger than us, and we often only see and know part of the bigger picture. It's why we are "sent out." There's a specific time and place and people that need the Holy Spirit's presence, and that presence resides in us!

Did you notice He said He sends us out like lambs among wolves? Isn't that comforting? Wow, great, ugh. We're often sent to places where we don't feel safe. For some, it may be on a stage or in a one-on-one gospel presentation. For others, it may be a new town or a new church. The scripture about lambs among wolves always concerned me until I realized that the wolf is already defeated, so the lamb can stroll through the wolf pack with no problem at all. We have nothing to fear because no weapon formed against us can prosper. So, we can go like a lamb through the wolves, and they can snarl all they want.

Then finally in this scripture it says, you will be set apart, you will be called out to a work, you will be sent out to a place, but then you will be "filled." The story in this scripture is actually kind of terrifying. Paul strikes a man with blindness, and it's a righteous thing. How many of you have had some believer strike you with blindness? That's kind of intense, isn't it? I'm wondering, how is this okay, but I look back in 2 Kings 6:18-19 about a man named Elisha, and when the enemy was coming against Elisha it says:

> When they came down to him, Elisha prayed to the Lord and said, "Strike this people with blindness, I pray." So He struck them with blindness according to the word of Elisha. Then Elisha said to them, "This is not the way, nor is this the city; follow me and I will bring you to the man whom you seek." And he brought them to Samaria.

At the words of Elisha, they were struck blind; and if we go back and study this, what happened was the enemy was coming against them. So, Elisha said, we've got to take them to the king. And so he blinds them, so that they will follow him to the king. They have no choice. They can't see. They follow him to the king. In front of the king they get their eyes opened up and they recognize who is king. It's a story about Jesus by the way. It’s about leading the blind to the King of Kings!

So Paul strikes Elymas blind, and this is the question I have when I read this story: what do you think made Paul believe that was the right thing to do? See Elymas is trying to keep the pro-counsel from coming to the faith by persuading him that Paul is not telling the truth, so if it were me, I'd be thinking, let's shut the guy's mouth. Let's make sure he doesn't speak so that he cannot convince the pro-counsel. Or maybe let's pull a Phillip on him and teleport him out of here! But I believe the answers to why Paul saw that as the best solution are in Acts 9. We see in Acts 9 that Paul is on his way to persecute the believers, and at this time he's called by his Jewish name, Saul. Paul is his Greek name, and he's traveling to put people in Damascus under arrest because of the Way. And we see in verses 3-9:

> As he was traveling, it happened that he was approaching Damascus, and suddenly a light from heaven flashed around him; and he fell to the ground and heard a voice saying to him, “Saul, Saul, why are you persecuting Me?” And he said, “Who are You, Lord?” And He *said*, “I am Jesus whom you are persecuting, but get up and enter the city, and it will be told you what you must do.” The men who traveled with him stood speechless, hearing the voice but seeing no one. Saul got up from the ground, and though his eyes were open, he could see nothing; and leading him by the hand, they brought him into Damascus. And he was three days without sight, and neither ate nor drank.

Do you remember what it said about Elymas when he was struck blind? He was looking for someone to lead him by the hand. Do you also remember what Saul said to Elymas? You'll be blind for a time. I think what's happening here is that Elymas is persecuting the gospel of Christ, and what was Saul doing when he was struck blind? He was persecuting the gospel of Christ. So why did Paul think the right thing to do was to strike him blind? I believe Paul remembered the love that God had for Saul when he blinded him. I believe that Paul remembered the directness of Jesus when Jesus said, why are you persecuting me? And although blindness was harsh, it was part of Saul's repentance process. This explanation put it in a whole new light for me. When I look at you Elymas, he says, you're doing wrong. Jesus told Saul, you're doing wrong. You'll be blind for a time. You'll be blind for three days. You're going to need to be led by the hand. As happened with Saul, your people will lead you by the hand into the city. But Saul knew at the end of that blindness there would be a beautiful restoration with the King. So he blinds Elymas and says, hey you're going to be blind for a while, and during that time, I intend for you to meet Jesus. Sometimes it may be hard for you so that you'll repent. Saul remembered what Jesus did for him, and he is attempting to do it for Elymas.

That's a hard thing to grasp of the loving Savior until we remember the Father's love and that sometimes discipline is in place because of love. It’s to save us from making the mistake again; to teach us, to train us. So Paul blinds because he remembers what blindness did for him. Paul was using something out of his own experience. We will often work in what we have already overcome. We will often be asked to work in an area that we have overcome. Often times, the one who heals was once sick, the one who encourages was once depressed, and the one who delivers was the one who was demonically oppressed. Don't think that God will not use what He has brought you through.

God will intervene with these kinds of issues with a temporary blindness when it's for His good. Let’s look at another example. I remember in scripture that the pro-counsel was being swayed away. It says that Elymas the magician was opposing them, seeking to turn the pro-counsel away from the faith. But after seeing Paul blind Elymas, it says, that then the pro-counsel believed when he saw what had happened, being amazed at the teaching of the Lord. In other words, the result of the demonstration of power brought the pro-counsel into belief.

And in 1 Corinthians 2:1-5, Paul says:

> And when I came to you, brethren, I did not come with superiority of speech or of wisdom, proclaiming to you the testimony of God. For I determined to know nothing among you except Jesus Christ, and Him crucified. I was with you in weakness and in fear and in much trembling, and my message and my preaching were not in persuasive words of wisdom, but in demonstration of the Spirit and of power, so that your faith would not rest on the wisdom of men, but on the power of God.

Paul says, I didn't try to use my words. I did not try to convince you of anything with my wisdom. I just wanted to demonstrate the power of God, so that your faith would not rest on the wisdom that I could pour out to you, but on the power of God. That's a profound statement. Paul is saying, "I could come to you and whip out that New Testament, and walk you through the Roman road. I can tell you how you're apart from Christ, and I can show you in scripture and deliver amazing wisdom. But I'd rather just heal deaf ears, heal blind eyes, and remove that cancer. "Because when we demonstrate God's power, then our faith in God does not rest upon the knowledge and wisdom of an argument. It rests on the demonstration of the power of the Spirit. Miracles are hard to forget. Arguments are not difficult to forget, but miracles remain."

Acts 1 and 2 shows us there was a baptism of the Spirit that happened on the day of Pentecost. Before that day (John 20), the disciples were in a room and Jesus came to them and and said, "peace be with you." And their response was, what, who are you? Then Jesus showed them the scars, and they said, "oh, it's Jesus," and they rejoiced! He said, peace be with you again, and breathed on them, and said receive the Holy Spirit. Then he said, I want you to go to Jerusalem because not many days from now, the Spirit will come upon you with power, as John had said, you'll be baptized in the Spirit.

But then scripture shows us in Acts that they were filled with the Spirit. After the initial baptism of the Spirit occurs at Pentecost, the disciples went on from that baptism and are filled with the Spirit. What is the difference in the filling and the baptism? I don't think that it's necessarily different from the baptism in the Spirit. I believe it's a manifestation of the baptism of the Spirit. When the Spirit comes upon us in the baptism of the Spirit, we are opened up to the power and significance of God, and things like the gifts of tongues, or prophecy or boldness may come upon us. If we look at other events of fillings, we see there were the same occurrences that happened at the baptism. Let me show you what I mean. In Acts 4:31:

> And when they had prayed, the place where they had gathered together was shaken, and they were all filled with the Holy Spirit and *began* to speak the word of God with boldness.

The Holy Spirit came and filled them, and they received boldness to speak the word of God. Acts 4:8:

> Then Peter, filled with the Holy Spirit, said to them, "Rulers and elders of the people, if we are on trial today for a benefit done to a sick man, as to how this man has been made well, let it be known to all of you and to all the people of Israel, that by the name of Jesus Christ the Nazarene, whom you crucified, whom God raised from the dead–by this name this man stands here before you in good health."

Again in Acts 13:52:

> And the disciples were continually filled with joy and with the Holy Spirit.

Again in Romans 15:18-19:

> For I will not presume to speak of anything except what Christ has accomplished through me, resulting in the obedience of the Gentiles by word and deed, in the power of signs and wonders, in the power of the Spirit;

> so that from Jerusalem and round about as far as Illyricum I have fully preached the gospel of Christ.

What is Peter saying here? He's saying that he's working, being filled by the power of the Spirit in the Gentile Kingdom.

Even Christ had to be filled with the spirit. In Luke 4:14-15:

> And Jesus returned to Galilee in the power of the Spirit, and news about Him spread through all the surrounding district. And He *began* teaching in their synagogues and was praised by all.

Acts 10:38:

> *You know of* Jesus of Nazareth, how God anointed Him with the Holy Spirit and with power, and *how* He went about doing good and healing all who were oppressed by the devil, for God was with Him.

If we need the Holy Spirit's power in our walk, and we're sharing the gospel, then we need to be filled with the Spirit! Without the power of the Spirit, all we have are words and words are often not enough. Although the word of God is powerful, even Paul said, if I try to convince you through scripture, then that's what your faith is based on; I'd rather you base your faith on the power of God.

Jesus was "set apart" in heaven. He was "called" to mankind. He was "sent out" to this earth and He was "filled" with the Spirit. We need those same things.

Why is this important? I believe there are people who are frustrated. From the time God called me in my living room in Flower Mound, Texas, it was three years before I stepped into a ministry position. It was three miserable years. Why, because I thought I was immediately ready. I knew I was ready, I was sure. I'd completely convinced myself that I was ready. I was ready to walk away from the job and take whatever salary He had for me because I just wanted to be in ministry, because I was ready. He had called me, and my desire was there, but the door was not opened yet. There were some bogus calls, but not yet the one he had for me. I spent three, very frustrating years waiting.

I would like to encourage and caution you. If you're waiting on the call, I know it's hard. I know it hurts, that it can be painful. I know you weep before God and say, “Come on, I'm ready!” That may be happening, but the place He's calling you to may not be ready for you, and He may need to get that place ready for you before He calls you. I believe this is what trips up most believers, some are afraid they're going to miss the call. “Did I get it already? God, what did I do wrong? Oh, was that something I was supposed to do? I'm not sure if I was supposed to. Well, maybe that was what I was supposed to do! Maybe I missed or overlooked something. So what am I supposed to do? I don't know!”

It doesn't happen that way. Why would God hide it under a bushel and see if we walk by and just happen to check under the bushel. When He's calling us to something where He wants the Spirit to go, it's not going to be a hidden mystery. What makes it a hidden mystery is our desire to find something that looks like a call so we can attach ourselves to it. It can be challenging to digest, but I've watched person, after person, after person pursue their own call in unsuccessful frustration. Why, because it never was the call of God on their life. They were not in line with the Spirit. They had an overwhelming desire that made sense to them. When the call comes, you'll know it. Why, because it will be in alignment with what's in your spirit. It will not be a secret, not even a debate, because He laid it in your heart and opened the door–you've been contemplating it. When it comes, you know, and there is no doubt. That's how people can leave jobs and go straight into ministry. It's how they can quit their job, go to school, to seminary, or whatever God's calling them to, without doubt. Why, because they know. I know because I got the call. I received the call in my home on Amhearst Lane in Flower Mound, Texas. The Spirit told me point blank, you will enter the King's service. For three years I looked at everything that came along, every opportunity, every teaching or music ministry opportunity, even things I didn't think I was qualified for. I wanted my name out there in case someone was looking for that guy that got called! I was desperate not to miss my calling.

But when the call came, it was not difficult to walk away from a six figure manufacturing job into a Baptist Church that needed a contemporary worship service. I watched God bless, and I found joy, even through some of the craziest religious people I had ever met.

I had joy because I knew I was right where He wanted me to be, doing what He wanted me to do, and that's what's going to happen for you. He wants us to be and stay at peace, and that's how we know. The same will happen for you if it has not already. The reason we feel that call is because there is a call there, but we wait. We wait, stay at peace, and are obedient in our hearts. Keep your heart pure. Don't get frustrated if somebody is put in a ministry before you. Don't get frustrated that God isn't working in your time. He is faithful, and He is doing what He said He would do.

I say this to encourage you, there is a call and you've been set apart. The Holy Spirit will send you out, and when He does, He will fill you with everything you need for it to be right. So relax, enjoy the wait, because when the wait is over, it's work. It'll be work that will bring you great joy while it feels consuming.

God loves you so much that he is preparing everything so that when you step into it, you'll know it's right. It will be hard, but it will be right. It's difficult to wait when the desire in your heart is to be used by God. It's a good desire, and right now you can best be used by God by keeping your heart pure, by keeping your heart open, by not getting frustrated with God. Don't get frustrated with His people. Keep your heart open to learn, to love, to grow, and to mature because right now you need to feel confident that He's getting the position ready for you. You feel ready, but the alignment hasn't come for where you're going. It could be that someone else is currently in the position He wants you in, or maybe He is bringing the afflicted, and they aren't there yet, but He is aligning the timing for everyone.

I want to pray with you if you are waiting on the call:

Father God, for this group of people that I know may be torn into knots inside, that have gotten so frustrated that they may even fear they've missed something. You're the God of the universe. How in the world could we miss it if you set it up? Maybe we were trying to make something work that wasn't it. God, I'm asking right now for a peace to come over them, that they are right where they're supposed to be, perfectly in the path on the journey. God, remind them that you are lining everything up. God, you are lining it up so that when you call, it will be the perfect fit, at the perfect time, and they will recognize it and know it. So I speak peace over you right now. Not just patience, but peace. I want you to have a burning desire in your heart, but I do not want you to be frustrated with God. The Holy Spirit will set you apart. He will call you, He will send you out and then He will fill you so that you can do the things that God has called you to do. Father God, give them assurance. Give them dreams in the middle of the night of the future of their ministry. Let them begin to see alignment, God, in things that You are lining up in their workplace, that You are lining up in their scripture reading, that You are lining up in their prayer time, that You are lining up with people around them. Bring Pastors into their life that will help line things up. Let them see the alignment so they have confidence that it's in the works God, because I know that if they can just see the plan unfolding, it's easier to go through the wait. Bless them with dreams, and bless them with visions. God, I thank you for a peace that passes all understanding, everything we don't understand. Bless them with strength in the waiting, maturity in the waiting, visions in the waiting, and words of assurance for them, in Jesus name. Amen.

Right now just receive a word from the Spirit about your ministry. Just be still and let Him give you a word about your ministry. Thank you Lord!

HOLY SPIRIT SEPARATION

This next chapter about Holy Spirit separation is pretty heavy, but really important. We are going to look at what it means to grieve the Holy Spirit. We could spend a pretty good portion of this chapter showing you scriptures that Holy Spirit is God, but we will look at one scripture for this, 2 Corinthians 3:17:

> Now the Lord is the Spirit, and where the Spirit of the Lord is, there is liberty.

We're going to be looking at what things grieve God and therefore grieve Holy Spirit because the Holy Spirit is the Lord. So lets start with Ephesians 4:30:

> Do not grieve the Holy Spirit of God, by whom you were sealed for the day of redemption.

Grieve in the Greek is "lypeo." And what "lypeo" means is to make sorrowful, to offend or to affect with sadness. In other words, bringing sadness upon Holy Spirit. And I just want to make the concept simple. So when we dig into this, we know what we're talking about. What happens in your relationship with your spouse or with your best friend when you have done something that makes them sad? What happens in a relationship when something is done to affect the other person in a way that makes them sad? Here are the things that happen when a separation begins. We do not communicate as much as we should or would have. There's a time of being apart emotionally. Maybe we don't share intimate things as much with each other. We are not close and we are separated even if we are physically in proximity. We are still in love, and we are still committed to one another, but because of the offense that's brought about sadness, there's a pulling away, there's a separation that happens in a relationship.

So when we talk about the Holy Spirit, I want this to be a baseline. I do not believe that the Holy Spirit is thin skinned. I do not believe that the Holy Spirit carries his feelings on his sleeves. I do not believe He is petty. I don't believe He is wimpy. I do not believe He gets his feelings hurt easily. I believe that the Holy Spirit is strong, fierce, authoritative and under the direction of God to guide and to teach us. He is determined, able, dedicated and yet has emotions, and can be saddened or grieved just as we can. I think too often when we talk about grieving the Holy Spirit, we begin to walk around on our tiptoes like, "Oh, I hope I didn't offend Him. I hope I didn't say something or He will go." I don't think it's like that. I think He's closer to us than that. I think He understands us better than to get pouty when things go wrong. But I think because of what He's called to do, He wants our attention. He wants our focus and He wants our response to Him. If we don't, if we grieve Him, there comes a time of separation, just like what happens with a loved one when we bring about sadness.

So I want you to consider this when we talk about what grieves the Holy Spirit. I think one of the easiest ways to determine what grieves the Holy Spirit is to talk about what the Holy Spirit's job is. What is his responsibility in our life? We need to understand the Holy Spirit's job is to teach us the deep things of God, 1 Corinthians 2. The Holy Spirit is to guide Christians into the truth, John 16, and to lead believers in their walk, Matthew 4. The Holy Spirit's job is to comfort when trials come, John 14, and to release special gifts to the believer, 1 Corinthians 14. And with these tasks at hand, what would grieve you if that was your job? If your job is to teach, to guide into the truth, to lead the believer, to comfort, and to release special gifting, what would grieve you?

Consider this, knowing that the Holy Spirit is God; lets go into scripture and look at the things that grieve God, and thus the Holy Spirit. Let's start in Genesis 6:5, which is in the time of Noah:

> Then the Lord saw that the wickedness of man was great on the earth, and that every intent of the thoughts of his heart was only evil continually. The Lord was sorry that He had made man on the earth, and He was grieved in His heart.

There are two words we can see in this scripture, the word *wickedness* and the word *evil*. Wickedness and evil were in the earth. In the Hebrew, the same word "ra" is used for both of those. Wickedness and evil are the same thing, just used in different contexts. Once used to say that "ra" was on the earth and then to say the thoughts of his heart were "ra," much like using the same word for a noun and then for a verb. The second thing He says is that the thoughts of man's heart were continually on evil. So, man's mind being on evil things grieves the Holy Spirit. Man's mind, soul and heart, dwelling on evil, grieves the Holy Spirit. If your mind is focused on pornography, it grieves the Holy Spirit because your thoughts are on evil. You should expect a separation from the Spirit during the times when you look at pornography.

So what is wicked, and what is evil? It's probably easiest for us to just make a list of what's evil and say, don't think about those things. We could talk about things like murder, rape, adultery, pornography, greed, and maybe hate. It would be easy to make these kinds of lists, but Jesus comes and He has us look from a different perspective. In Matthew 9:2-4 he says this:

> And they brought to Him a paralytic lying on a bed. Seeing their faith, Jesus said to the paralytic, "Take courage son; your sins are forgiven." And some of the scribes said to themselves, "This fellow blasphemes." And Jesus knowing their thoughts said, "Why are you thinking evil in your hearts?"

Evil is being defined here as not believing Jesus is who he says he is and that Jesus can do what he says he can do. Evil is defined as believing Jesus was blaspheming God. In Matthew 12:38:

> Then some of the scribes and Pharisees said to him, "Teacher, we want to see a sign from you." But he answered and said, "An evil and adulterous generation craves for a sign; and yet no sign will be given to it but the sign of Jonah the prophet."

Here, Jesus defines evil as when they wanted to base whether or not they would believe on whether or not they would see something miraculous. There are people who chase the miraculous to build their faith. I call them "river jumpers." Always looking for a new river, a place to go where something miraculous might happen to build their faith. Scripture says that signs follow those who believe. So you build your faith, and those signs follow your faith. We get it backward, and Jesus says it's evil.

When we look at Genesis 6:11, God describes what's going on in the earth at that time. He says:

> Now the earth was corrupt in the sight of God, and the earth was filled with violence.

This is really interesting because this word violence in the Hebrew, and some of you will get this right away, is hamas. Hamas was on the earth in those days and hamas in the Hebrew means wrong, cruelty, injustice, damage, unrighteousness and falsehood. I don't know about you, but when we're talking about the Holy Spirit (God) being grieved by these things, I look at what's opposite of those things to determine what keeps the Holy Spirit from being grieved.

When scripture talks about the fruits of the Spirit, they are love, joy, peace, patience, kindness, goodness, faithfulness, gentleness and self-control. So when evil enters our lives, it produces the opposite of what the Holy Spirit wants to put in our life and therefore He is grieved. So evil in our life grieves the Holy Spirit.

If we go into Galatians 5, where the fruits of the Spirit are listed, He gives the antonym of the fruit. In verse 19- 21 he says:

> Now the deeds of the flesh,

The Holy Spirit is spirit, and these are deeds of the *flesh*. The things of the flesh are not of the spirit, therefore not things of the Holy Spirit. I want to go over the definition based on this long list of deeds of the flesh. We will look at the Greek definition and how Paul is using it in this list.

He starts with the word **immorality**, which in the Greek is porneia. Does this sound familiar? It means *immorality, pornea, pornography, any sex outside of marriage and adultery.*

The next word is **impurity**, which in the Greek means *improper motives*. The opposite of this word is actually holiness.

Next on the list is **sensuality** which is *shamelessness; indecent body movement and filthy words fall under sensuality.*

Next is **idolatry**, which is *the worship of anything that's not God, including money and self.*

Sorcery, is the *administration of drugs, addiction, poisoned, magical arts of the occult*.

Enmity, hatred and hostility is *bitterness toward somebody.*

Strife is *people who are quarrelling debaters and contentious*.

Jealousy is *envying.*

Outbursts of anger, which speaks for itself.

Disputes. This is interesting in the Greek. Disputes means to *put yourself forward, in other words, whatever it takes to get me ahead*.

Dissension means to *create division over*. In other words "Let's argue doctrine. Let's argue theology. Let's create dissension based on thought."

Factions are *creating disunity in people, separating people*.

Envying, which is *creating ill will as a distraction*.

Drunkenness, which means being intoxicated.

Orgies, which are group sex.

This is just a short list of things that will separate you from Holy Spirit. But let's look at something else besides this list that the Bible says grieves Holy Spirit. It's in Psalms 95:8-10 which says:

> Do not harden your hearts, as at Meribah, as in the day of Massah in the wilderness,

Now what does Meribah and Massah mean in the scripture? Meribah and Massah are places between Egypt and the promised land, between Egypt and Israel. These were places they had journeyed, and He said, don't harden your heart like they did there. Now continue:

> "When your fathers tested Me, they tried Me, though they had seen My work. For 40 years I loathed that generation and said they are a people who err in their heart, and they do not know My ways."

There are two things He says about them that made Him loath, that made that generation separate from Him. First, they strayed in their hearts. In scripture, the heart, soul, and mind are all referring to the same part of man. So He's saying they strayed in their thinking by not transforming themselves by the renewing of their minds. They didn't stay focused on Him. They went astray in their thinking. And secondly, He says they do not know my "ways." By ways, I believe He is saying that they must learn the character of God if they are to interpret and use the word of God.

Then He makes this statement that I thought was interesting, "they tried Me, though they had seen My work." They questioned God even though they'd seen Him come through time after time. They were miraculously delivered out of Egypt, then they still said, "Yeah, but where is God?" Let me tell you how I see this playing out in the church today. “God, why did you let this terrible thing happen to me?” HE DIDN’T! It infuriates me when people blame God for something the devil did. I believe the devil laughs when we blame God for what our enemy did. The devil must be saying, “I messed you up, and you blamed God for it. I win twice!”

Maybe what we should learn is that oftentimes the enemy has a right to us because we keep sticking our foot in sin and then wondering why God didn't protect us from the ramifications. We grieve the Holy Spirit when we don't know the ways of God. This is really critical, He did not say they don't know the Law of God, He said they don't know His ways. They don't know how or why He does things or the purpose for the way He does them. I believe it really grieves the Holy Spirit that we don't know the ways of God because we are looking for God to be our sugar daddy. “Just give us things God, just give things to us. That's how I know you love me. Just give to me.” We want the blessings of God without obedience to God. We want sin in our life, and we want God to bless us at the same time. “I want God, but I'm looking at porn. I want God, but I'm sleeping with someone I'm not married to. I want God, but only when I need something, otherwise don't bother me. I want God, but I don't give a dime to The Kingdom. I want God, but I refuse to speak about Him in public. I want God, but I drink too much. I want God, but I don't spend any time with Him except at church.” Here's the problem, we don't want to worship God; we want God to worship us. Here's how it plays out, “God, if you take care of my problems, I will serve you. If you prove your love for me, then I will show you affection. God, you must answer all questions to my satisfaction if you expect my loyalty.” What we are doing is asking God to worship us. I believe scripture tells us that God told Job exactly why it is the other way around. See, we want the benefits of God without the loyalty, without the purity, without the holiness, without the justice, without giving, without the sacrifice on our part because we want to live under grace and try to take advantage of it.

We don't know God’s ways; we don’t even know Him. We know that He's merciful, but we forget He doesn't tolerate sin. We know that He’s loving, but He’s also jealous of our loyalty. We know that He's miraculous, but He requires faith. We understand that He's generous, but He's demanding of our offering. We know that He's omnipresent, but He doesn't control us. We know that He has plans for us, but we can choose to reject them. So we need to understand the ways of God; how He fathers us, how a father does what's best for us, wants to develop us, wants to mature us, and wants to help us learn to think. We've got to know His ways, not just live under His rules.

Let's look at another thing that grieves the Spirit. Isaiah 43:24 says:

> "You have bought Me not sweet cane with money, nor have you filled Me with the fat of your sacrifices; Rather you have burdened Me with your sins, you have wearied Me with your iniquities."

There is a difference between sin and iniquity. Sin is defined by the Law, by the over 600 rules that we followed and the 10 commandments. The law is a tutor for us; it defines what sin is. So we know what sin is when we break the Law, but here He also says, you've wearied me with your iniquities. What's our iniquity? Iniquity is what causes us to *choose sin*. It's that thing inside of us that's broken that we don't address, and it allows us to choose sin when we don't fix the iniquity. It's that selfish desire inside that says, "I will do what I want." That's the iniquity. I haven't sinned yet, but the iniquity in my heart says I'm going to sin to meet my needs. It's sometimes our belief, which is actually a lie of the enemy that has been planted in us. We believe the lie, and it's not the truth because it does not measure up against the word of God. We make decisions to sin based on the iniquity of that lie in our life. Sin is our decision to go against the instructions of God and it grieves the Holy Spirit, and iniquity is our desire to please ourselves, and it also grieves Holy Spirit.

The most graphic picture we have of sorrow in the entire scripture is in the garden of Gethsemane. Scripture says when Jesus prayed, His sorrow was so great that His sweat dropped like blood. I don't mind saying this, but in the year 2000 I went through a very sorrowful time, and there was a moment that what had just happened really struck me. And when it did, I begin to weep. I wept with such a sorrow that I could not breathe. You know what I'm talking about, right? Your face turns red and you can't breathe. Do you know what happens if you can't catch your breath? The corpuscles in your face break and your face starts to bleed when you're so intensely involved in this sorrow. It ends up busting the corpuscles in your face. I had that experience, but mine didn't drop like blood, it broke out like a bloody rash on my face and I knew if I didn't get a breath, it was going to turn into what happened in the garden.

There was such a great grief in the garden over the sin of man and over what Jesus was about to have to go through. Jesus was realizing the cup would not pass him and that the very wrath of God would be poured out on him because of the sin of man. He was grieved over it. He was loyal, dedicated, loving, committed, but grieved. This is the grief of our Lord.

Another scripture that declares what grieves the Holy Spirit, is in Isaiah 63:10 it says:

> But they rebelled and grieved his Holy Spirit;
> Therefore, he turned Himself to become their enemy,
> He fought against them.

They were disobedient. They didn't want to do what God had asked them to do. They *decided* to be disobedient. This grieved the Holy Spirit. For us, disobedience is disobedience to the logos word of God *and* disobedience to the rhema word of God. What does this mean? It means that I can understand in scripture the things I need to be obedient to, but when He tells me in the grocery store to go pray for that woman and I don't, that I'm being disobedient to the rhema word of God. He tells us that their disobedience caused His grief and then God began to work against them. Now, I need you to hear me on this really closely. If you understand the ways of God, God is not angry. God is not trying to punish. God is trying to bring about repentance so He's working against them so they cannot succeed in their disobedience; then they will have to turn back to God and say, “We rebelled and were disobedient. We want reconciliation with you.” It’s called repentance, knowing God's ways, that He is not mean or their enemy; He's trying to get them to turn back to Him.

Finally, I want to go back to the first scripture where we started because anytime we read something that says, don't grieve the Holy Spirit, there must be a conversation around it that would help us understand that grieving. So let's go back to Ephesians 4:25-32:

> Therefore, laying aside falsehood, speak truth each one of you with his neighbor, for we are members of one another. Be angry, and yet do not sin.

That's a confusing one for a lot of people. You can go back to our Hide and Seek book that was previously published to learn about righteous anger versus unrighteous anger. Jesus was righteously angry in the temple when he turned over the money changers' tables in the temple, but there is also an unrighteous anger that is sinful. So we have to know when to be angry and what to be angry about or it can be sinful. Ephesians 4:26-29 says:

> Be angry, and yet do not sin; do not let the sun go down on your anger, and do not give the devil an opportunity. He who steals must steal no longer; but rather he must labor, performing with his own hands what is good, so that he will have something to share with one who has a need.

Now this is a crusher.

> Let no unwholesome word proceed from your mouth.

Just review what you have spoken in the last seven days. Have we spoken anything in the last seven days that was unwholesome? You might wonder, "Well, how would I know if it was unwholesome?" We can tell by reading the rest of the verse:

> But only such a word as is good for edification according to the need of the moment, so that it will give grace to those who hear.

Let me reword that for you. What Paul's saying is that instead of speaking unwholesomely, I want you to build each other up with the love of God. Have my words been unwholesome and therefore grieving the Holy Spirit, or have they been words of love to edify and build up others? Then verse 30:

> Do not grieve the Holy Spirit of God, by whom you were sealed for the day of redemption. Let all bitterness and wrath and anger and clamor and slander be put away from you, along with all malice. Be kind to one another, tenderhearted, forgiving each other, just as God in Christ also has forgiven you.

Paul starts the conversation by saying, get rid of falsehood, anger, theft and unwholesome words. Then he said, don't grieve the Holy Spirit, and comes right back with, watch for bitterness, wrath, anger, clamor, slander and malice. Put those things away from you. He's reaffirming with more specific words that he needs these things out of our lives; these are things that grieve the Spirit. But then he ends this way in verse 32, which I think is beautiful. He says, be kind to one another, tender hearted and forgiving each other just as God in Christ has forgiven you. In other words, there will never be a time when it grieves the Holy Spirit that you were kind, loving, tenderhearted or forgiving to somebody. I don't think the Holy Spirit will ever stop and say, “Stop being so nice!” Instead, just be forgiving. You were forgiven, so be forgiving. We're not talking about losing our salvation or removing the seal that has been set in place for the day of redemption by the Spirit within us by grieving the Spirit. What we are saying is that we can bring sadness to the Spirit, and He will back away from us.

But here is the main point; the very essence of the everlasting holiness of God dwells in us! So why would we choose the things of death to come join with us? These things can't live together. Grieving the Holy Spirit occurs when we have holiness in us (the Holy Spirit) *AND* we invite sin to come in. This grieves the Holy Spirit.

To end, let’s look at a scripture, it’s in the book of Exodus, chapter 23. God is telling Joshua about how he's going to lead the people into the Promised Land. How does that apply to us? When we come to know Christ as our Savior, we enter our promised land, which is the Kingdom of God. How do we know our promised land is the Kingdom of God and not heaven? When they stepped over into their promised land, they had to do battle to claim the territory and drive an enemy out. When we step into the Kingdom of God, we have to do battle to drive the enemy out and claim the territory. In the Kingdom of Heaven, there is no enemy to drive out; but in the Kingdom of God, since we are still on this earth, we are equipped, but we battle the enemy in our territories. The Old Covenant stories are a physical representation of the spiritual concepts of the New Covenant.

So watch this happen in *Exodus* 23:20:

> Behold, I am going to send an angel before you to guard you along the way and to bring you into the place which I have prepared.

In that time it was an angel that got sent before them to go into the land, but for us, it's the Holy Spirit; so if we read it again in that context:

> Behold, I am going to send an angel before you to guard you along the way and to bring you into the place that I have prepared.

Who convicts us of sin to enter the Kingdom of God? The Holy Spirit leads us into a place that God has prepared for us, the Kingdom of God.

> Be on your guard before him and obey his voice; do not be rebellious toward him.

We just talked about disobedience and rebellion, grieving the Spirit.

> Do not be rebellious toward him, for he will not pardon your transgressions, since My name is in him.

Whoa, what just happened here, He doesn't forgive sins? That doesn't sound like New Covenant stuff. It's because we don't understand the word pardon in the Hebrew, the word pardon in the Hebrew is “nasa” which means “to carry.” He will not carry our sins for us. In other words, if we go pick up a sin, He's going to back out and let us carry it. He's going to separate from us because He’s not going to carry sin. In other words, He is not going to put up with the sin that we're carrying in our life. Let's go on,

> But if you truly obey his voice and do all that I say,

The Holy Spirit doesn't speak unless he hears God speak. So if we obey Him, what we're doing is what God says:

> But if you truly obey his voice and do all that I say, then I will be an enemy to your enemies and an adversary to your adversaries. For My angel will go before you and bring you into the land of the Amorites, the Hittites, the Perizzites, the Canaanites, the Hivites and the Jebusites; and I will completely destroy them. You shall not worship their gods, nor serve them, nor do according to their deeds; but you shall utterly overthrow them and break their sacred pillars in pieces.

That's our job in the Kingdom of God, to overthrow the enemy working in our territory, to destroy the tools that the enemy is using to destroy the land.

> But you shall serve the Lord your God, and He will bless your bread and your water; and I will remove sickness from your midst. There shall be no one miscarrying or barren in your land; I will fulfill the number of your days.

What he just said was this: I'm sending the Holy Spirit ahead of you into the promised land, in the Kingdom of God. Don't grieve the Spirit. Listen to him. Don't rebel against the Spirit. He will stay with you. And if you stay with Holy Spirit and you get rid of all of this evil and wickedness that's in the land, then I will bless you. So that's where we are as believers. This is what happens, we look at our lives and we wonder why we're not blessed. And often the reason is because the Holy Spirit has withdrawn Himself from us because of sin we've allowed into our life. This is not meant as a rebuke, but is truth. If we can go in and identify the sin that is in our life and get it out of our life, the Holy Spirit is no longer grieved and He steps in to bless us! So if we want the blessing of God, and we're not getting it, we need to look at where the rebellion, sin, or disobedience is and say, "I'm done with that because I want the blessing of God." I believe that we are in a time right now where God wants to release a great move of Holy Spirit, and He is waiting for us to go consecrate ourselves and remove the things in our life that shouldn't be there, the things that are grieving Him.

Pornography must be addressed if we want to be blessed by the Holy Spirit. Do you want to see someone healed? Do you want to see someone delivered? Do you want to see someone come to Christ? Do you want God to bless you and your family? Do you want Him to bless you in your job and your finances? And yet you want to look at porn? It does not work that way, it will not work, it cannot work! Try Him in this, go ahead and kick that stuff out of your life. Be done with it and watch the flood gates of blessing open up!

This is not a chapter about pornography. This is a chapter about the evilness and the wickedness we are currently letting into our lives and saying it's just our society, it's normal. We just put up with watching that on TV. We just put up with those kinds of attitudes. We just put up with that kind of tolerance because the enemy tells us that unless we are tolerant about what others are doing, we are hateful, and that's not true. The truth is, that because I love you, I don't want you to suffer what will happen because of sin in your life.

We are on the verge! We have the opportunity to move in a great way in the Spirit, but it's going to take all of us stepping back and saying, "Where did I put my foot in evil? Where have I opened the door to wickedness? Where am I disobedient to God? I will no longer grieve the Holy Spirit. I'm going to ask Him to draw in close and bless me because I'm going to drive that darkness out so that I have room for Him to come in. The Holy Spirit is free to move in my life!!"

Father God, we are looking for consecration. We want the enemy out of our camp and we want Holy Spirit totally in. We apologize and we repent. We want a strong blessing relationship with you, so even now as you bring it to our mind, whatever it is, we lay it at the foot of the cross and we say, forgive us for that. Give us strength. Let us walk away from that and towards your embrace. We love you, Holy Spirit. We do not want to grieve you. Teach us the truth in Jesus name. Amen!

HOLY SPIRIT PRODUCTION

When we talk about the Holy Spirit and production, we're talking about what the Bible calls fruit, and fruit produces fruit. From the very beginning, the beauty of fruit is that it reproduces itself. God said He made all of these trees that grow, and they have seed bearing fruit that they produce. As they produce fruit, that fruit can regenerate another tree and produce more fruit. So the fruit that is produced by a tree guarantees that fruit will continue to be produced by trees from that fruit. Make sense? It's a self perpetuating, never-ending cycle, and we can start in a popular scripture regarding fruit in Galatians 5:13-26:

> For you were called to freedom brethren; only do not turn freedom into an opportunity for the flesh, but through love serve one another. For the whole law is fulfilled in one word, in the statement, "You shall love your neighbor as yourself." But if you bite and devour one another, take care that you are not consumed by one another. But I say, walk by the Spirit, and you will not carry out the desire of the flesh. For the flesh sets its desire against the Spirit, and the Spirit against the flesh; for these are in opposition to one another, so that you may not do the things that you please.
>
> But if you are led by the Spirit, you are not under the Law. Now, the deeds of the flesh are evident, which are; immorality, impurity, sensuality, idolatry, sorcery, enmities, strife, jealousy, outbursts of anger, disputes, dissensions, factions, envying, drunkenness, carousing and things like these, of which I forewarn you, just as I have forewarned you, that those who practice such things will not inherit the Kingdom of God.

> But the fruit of the Spirit is love, joy, peace, patience, kindness, goodness, faithfulness, gentleness, self-control; against such things there is no law. Now those who belong to Christ Jesus have crucified the flesh with its passions and desires. If we live by the Spirit, let us also walk by the Spirit. Let us not become boastful, challenging one another, envying one another.

So when I read this scripture, what I find out is that there are fruits that indicate whether or not we are walking by the Spirit. There is a list of fruit that would indicate that if I'm walking by the Spirit, these things should be produced. I want to tell you something I found that was really unique in verse 25, "if we live by the Spirit, let us also walk by the Spirit." Do you know what? If you go into the Greek, the words "by the" are not in the original Greek text. Those are words inserted by translators to help explain. So the actual text says, "If we live Spirit, let us walk Spirit." Did you get that? "If we live spirit, let us walk Spirit." I like that; I think it's a better interpretation.

Verse 18 says, "but if you are led by the Spirit, you are not under the Law." Now, let's look at that from a very practical standpoint. If we are led by the Spirit, we're not under the Law. A baseline theological statement would indicate that if the Spirit is in us and we are being led by the Spirit, then we have come to know Christ. Therefore, the Spirit has indwelled us, and we have been set free from the curse of the Law. We are not under the Law anymore because we are under Christ. We cannot be under the Law *AND* be led by the Spirit because being indwelled by the Spirit, being *'in Christ,'* takes us out from under the Law. For anyone who has not come to know Christ as Savior, and has not accepted what He's done, is actually still under the Law. This is why scripture says not one jot or tittle of the Law will go away until all is fulfilled, because we need the Law to define sin. Sin has to be defined, so that we know we are lost. Once we know we are lost, we can accept Christ as our Savior. Does this make sense?

This is partially why the Spirit and the Law are actually in opposition to one another. Consider this, the Spirit wants you to love, show mercy, and seek justice. The Law wants to define your sin so that you can be condemned by it. The Law actually looks for you to follow the passions of the flesh so that you can commit lawlessness, thus commit the sin. The Spirit wants you to walk in righteousness so as to obtain abundant life. This is why verse 17 says, "for the flesh sets its desire against the Spirit, and the Spirit against the flesh; for these are in opposition to one another, so that you may not do the things that you please."

Here's another way to look at walking by the Spirit versus being under the Law. When we walk by the Spirit, we are not under the Law because when we walk by the Spirit, we are no longer making decisions based on a set of rules. Be sure to stay with me, I'm not saying the rules (the Law) are invalid. What I am saying, is that we are not making our decisions based on being bound to a Law, and we no longer make decisions for the sake of keeping the Law. *We are bound to a walk that is guided by the Spirit*, not by a set of rules. The best way for me to say this is that we mature from the place of "*keeping rules*" that we used to be under to "*applying wisdom we learned from the rules*." Let me say that again; we mature from "keeping rules" to "applying wisdom learned from the rules" that we were under. Galatians 3:23 says it this way:

> But before faith came, we were kept in custody under the law, being shut up to the faith which was later to be revealed. Therefore the Law has become our tutor to lead us to Christ, so that we may be justified by faith. But now that faith has come, we are no longer under a tutor. For you are all sons of God through faith in Christ Jesus.

This is a beautiful statement in understanding the Law for the believer. The Law has to be in place to identify sin, and if we do not accept Christ as our Savior, then we will stand before God trying to justify ourselves by the Law, by the over 600 rules. If we say, "did I ever break one of these?" Yes we did. And if we broke one, then we're condemned guilty of all of them the Bible says. But if we accept Christ as our own Lord and Savior, then He has made atonement for our sin, He has given us a remittance for that sin. He has redeemed us from the Law so that we might stand before God as righteous in Him. Let's look at how Jesus showed us how to apply "under the Spirit" as opposed to being "under the Law," in Matthew 5:27-28:

> You have heard that it was said, 'you shall not commit adultery,' but I say to you that everyone who looks at a woman with lust for her has already committed adultery with her in his heart. If your right eye makes you stumble, tear it out and throw it from you; for it is better for you to lose one of the parts of your body, than for your whole body to be thrown into hell.

What is Matthew saying? He's saying listen, here was the rule, don't sleep with her. That's the rule–don't sleep with her. And if you do, then you have broken the Law, if you do, then you are condemned. But Jesus says, this is what I'm going to tell you. Instead of worrying about breaking the rule, recognize the process that leads you to breaking the rule. I'm going to lead you by the Spirit to say watch what your eyes see, because your eyes can lead you into a temptation. When you start to look upon her with lust, that's the beginning of the process, that's the first step. You will need to examine your heart to find out why you are looking at her in that way. So I want you to know the rule, but you need to be careful way back here at the lust stage. You need to be careful with what your eyes are seeing.

So nip that thing in the bud before the destruction of your marriage, the destruction of your family, or the destruction of your own life starts. Recognize that there used to be a rule, but we don't want to get near breaking the rule, we want to walk in an upright way prior to that. The Spirit will guide you away from looking, thus saving your destruction. But with the Law it says, we'll wait until you've committed adultery so that you can be condemned. Why, because we have to commit a sin for the Law to have value. If we don't commit a sin, then we have not transgressed the Law and the Law does not have an effect, because we haven't broken a rule. Does that make sense? The Law requires a sin before it has value, but the Spirit prevents us from entering the condemnation process that the Law will bring.

Another thing to notice is the comparison in this scripture of the "works of the flesh" and the "fruit of the Spirit." "Works" of the flesh are not compared to "works" of the Spirit because there are no "works of the Spirit," nor are there "fruits of the flesh." There are only "works of the flesh." And what the Spirit produces is "fruit" not "works." That's going to mean so much in a minute, the Spirit does not produce works in us. The Spirit produces fruit in us. The comparison is the Law against the Spirit. In order to keep from breaking the Law, we must work in our effort. Do not sleep with her. In this, we're working with our own effort. The Spirit is in opposition to the Law, so anything in our effort is against the Spirit. But now you're probably thinking: well shouldn't I work to be kind and loving and peaceful?

Let's look at the fruit of the Spirit, let's look at the fruit in this list because I think there's a unique thing that we'll see as we go through it. The first fruit is Love. We know from scripture that God is love. And the word used here is agape, which is a full on, full fledged, full love from the heart. Are we capable of this kind of love in our works? No. This kind has to come from inside, there must be a source for this kind of love that is beyond what we are capable of. The next fruit is Joy. The Joy of the Lord is my strength. This joy is an attribute of God. Next, peace, biblically I can have a peace that goes beyond my understanding, and Jesus is the prince of peace. And the next is patience. And listen, patience is not the ability to wait, that's not what patience is. Patience is the ability to lack, and to be at peace with it. It's being steadfast, and slow to avenge wrongs. Then there is kindness, and kindness is a moral goodness and integrity. It is your kindness, Lord, that leads us to repentance. Then goodness, and goodness is being upright in heart and life. And faithfulness, which is the conviction of what is true. And gentleness, which is a mild disposition, being meek. Jesus is meek and humble in heart, Matthew 11:29. And finally self-control, which is the ability to master emotions and do what's called for instead of being out of control.

So here's the point, this list is not a list of works, and did you notice a common theme when you went through these? These are attributes that the Lord shows us about Himself. They are attributes of the Lord, that He is Loving, that He is Joy, that He is Peace. It's His Love, His Joy, His Peace. He is the Prince of Peace, and it's His Kindness that leads us to repentance. It's His Faithfulness to us. These are attributes of the Lord Himself, *AND* they are evidences of the Spirit of God in us. When we put these together, these attributes of Him, the Spirit of God who lives in us; these attributes can live in us! It's not what we produce, it's what the Holy Spirit is producing in us.

For these to be present, the Holy Spirit must be present because they are the fruit He produces. They are the fruit "of the Holy Spirit," not the fruit of man! We don't seem to have any problem understanding that there are gifts of the Spirit. We believe that the Spirit gives us gifts. We believe that we operate in a gift that He has given to us, and yet this scripture talks about the fruit of the Spirit. So it's NOT OUR FRUIT. It is His fruit that He is producing in us. Stay with me. Listen to this scripture in Galatians 2:16:

> Nevertheless knowing that a man is not justified by the works of the Law but through faith in Christ Jesus, even we have believed in Christ Jesus, so that we may be justified by faith in Christ and not by the works of the Law; since by the works of the Law, no flesh will be justified.

So maybe it's not about us becoming more loving people. It's not about becoming more peaceful people, or about becoming more gentle people, but becoming a people who walk by the Spirit, so the Spirit can produce His fruit in us.

Man is trying to be justified by works, but the works of man are of himself. If we are trying to do things on our own, then it would be works. This would put us back under the Law, trying to prove to God that we can be loving, gentle, and peaceful, trying to merit God's favor by what we do. It's about walking in the Spirit so that Holy Spirit's fruit is produced in us. Now that we have this concept, we have also heard of this concept in another context. In John 15:5, let's apply what we're talking about in the Spirit and fruit.

> I am the vine, you are the branches; he who abides in Me and I in him, he bears much fruit, for apart from Me you can do nothing.

What's the context of the conversation in which you can do nothing? Producing fruit. So here's what He's saying: I abiding in you will produce fruit. If I am not abiding in you, you cannot produce fruit. In the same way, the fruit of the Spirit is fruit from the Holy Spirit. If we walk in Him, His fruit gets produced. Apart from the Holy Spirit, you cannot produce the "fruit of the Spirit." Remember, if we live by the Spirit, let us also walk by the Spirit! I'm not saying we can't be kind without the Holy Spirit, what I am saying is, we will have to produce these things on our own, by our own works. That's different from having them produced for us by the Spirit. So the big question is, "Are we producing love, joy, peace, patience, kindness, goodness, faithfulness, gentleness, self control or is the Holy Spirit producing them because He is walking with us and in us. I don't know about you, but that takes a lot of pressure off me. The pressure for me to try to be good, to try to be right, and to try to do right things because it is not a fruit that I'm producing; it's a fruit that He's producing in me.

Now the Bible also talks about the fact that we can produce bad fruit outside of the Holy Spirit. Let's look at three examples. Matthew 7:15, I'll call it the fruit of false inspiration. In another chapter we talked about inspiration. We talked about the very rhema word of God, that breath of God through us. But this scripture in Matthew 7:15-23 says:

> "Beware of the false prophets, who come to you in sheep's clothing, but inwardly are ravenous wolves. You will know them by their fruits. Grapes are not gathered from thorn bushes nor figs from thistles, are they? So every good tree bears good fruit, but the bad tree bears bad fruit. A good tree cannot produce bad fruit, nor can a bad tree produce good fruit. Every tree

> that does not bear good fruit is cut down and thrown into the fire." So then, you will know them by their fruits.:"
>
> "Not everyone who says to me, 'Lord, Lord,' will enter the Kingdom of Heaven, but he who does the will of my Father who is in heaven will enter. And many will say to me on that day, 'Lord, Lord, did we not prophesy in Your name and in Your name cast out demons, and in Your name perform many miracles? And I will declare to them, 'I never knew you; depart from Me, you who practice lawlessness.'"

Listen, a good tree cannot produce bad fruit. That's an amazing statement. A good tree filled with the Spirit cannot produce bad fruit, nor can a bad tree produce good fruit. Now lets go back, because there's a really concerning statement for people. What happens if I get to heaven and he says, "I don't know you?" Go back to the beginning of the scripture, "beware of the false prophets." Lord, didn't we prophesy in Your name? No, you did not prophesy in My name, you are a false prophet. False prophets do not have the Holy Spirit living in them. False prophets try to produce a work of prophesy in and of themselves. Therefore, the false prophet cannot produce good fruit because it's not the Holy Spirit that's producing that fruit.

Matthew 12:33-34 is what we'll call the fruit of an evil heart.

> Either make the tree good and its fruit good or make the tree bad and its fruit bad; for the tree is known by its fruit. You brood of vipers. How can you, being evil, speak what is good? For the mouth speaks out of that which fills the heart. The good man brings out of his good treasure what is good; and the evil man brings out of his evil treasure what is evil.

If your heart is bad, you are not walking by the Spirit. Luke 6:39-45, I'll call this the fruit of hypocrisy, the bad fruit of hypocrisy.

> And He also spoke a parable to them: A blind man cannot guide a blind man, can he? Will they not both fall into a pit? A pupil is not above his teacher; but everyone, after he has been fully trained, will be like his teacher. Why do you look at the speck that is in your brother's eye, but do not notice the log that is in your own eye? Or how can you say to your brother, 'Brother, let me take out the speck that is in your eye' when you yourself do not see the log that is in your own eye? You hypocrite. First take the log out of your own eye, and then you will see clearly to take out the speck that is in your brother's eye. For there is no good tree which produces bad fruit, nor, on the other hand, a bad tree which produces good fruit. For each tree is known by its fruit. For men do not gather figs from thorns, nor do they pick grapes from a brier bush. The good man out of the good treasure of his heart brings forth what is good; and the evil man out of the evil treasure brings forth what is evil; for his mouth speaks from that which fills his heart.

Are you seeing this repetitive theme about fruit? I'm not skipping through the gospels to give you the same story out of multiple gospels, these are all out of Matthew. This is the third time he has told us that a tree will be known by its fruit. The work of trying to point out others' error, instead of working on your own, is walking in works not in the Spirit.

We can measure whether or not the Holy Spirit is in something based on the fruit that it produces. Let's be very blunt here, if you ever want to be a Pastor, you must learn this. You must learn that you will recognize the Holy Spirit in a person based on their fruit. If the fruit they produce creates division in the church body, it's not of the Spirit. If their fruit produces pride, it's not of the Spirit. If the fruit produces things of the flesh and immorality, impurity, sensuality, idolatry, sorcery, enmity, strife, jealousy, outbursts of anger, disputes, dissensions, factions, envying, drunkenness, carousing and things like that, it's not of the Spirit.

This is really important, if someone is creating factions in the church body, it is not of the Spirit, that fruit is not of unity. It's not holy, and it's not of the Holy Spirit. However, if they produce the fruit of the Holy Spirit, if they produce love, joy, peace, patience, kindness, goodness, faithfulness gentleness and self-control, then the Holy Spirit is in them! You may not even like it, but the Holy Spirit is in it. So here's the bottom line, we must become fruit inspectors!

Time after time, after time, after time, I've seen people trying to do a good work, but it produces bad fruit. Why? Because the Spirit was not in it, it was a work of the flesh. It was accomplished by passion, it was what they wanted, it was what they thought was good. Watch this, it comes from what they think will give them credit before God by doing something good. But that's the Law, straight up the Law! They want to do something so God will approve of them. But we are under Christ, therefore we are led by the Spirit. We are not trying to prove to God that we can be good. We should be allowing God to produce through us so that we are good!

If we are doing things out of our flesh, we can expect bad fruit. We need to check ourselves. We're not only inspecting what we see in others, we're inspecting what's coming out of us! Our passion may tell us this is the right thing to do, but if it creates division or pride, it's *NOT* of the Spirit! It's a hard lesson to learn. So when we see bad fruit in our lives, we need to stop it! Stop doing what we're doing because it's creating division, and it's creating pride in us, period. It's creating a problem, and it's not a fruit of the Spirit.

Because I love connecting the Old Testament to the New Testament, lets look at this concept in the book of Leviticus. In Leviticus 26:3-6 God says:

> If you walk in My statutes and keep My commandments so as to carry them out, then I shall give you rains in their season, so that the land will yield its produce and the trees of the field will bear their fruit. Indeed, your threshing will last for you until grape gathering, and the grape gathering will last until sowing time. You will thus eat your food to the full and live

> securely in your land. I shall also grant peace in the land, so that you may lie down with no one making you tremble. I shall also eliminate harmful beasts from the land, and no sword will pass through your land.

What are rains in scripture? Rains are the Spirit. God says I will give you the Holy Spirit in the season, so that the land will yield its produce and the trees of the field will bear their fruit. Why will they bear fruit? Because, they have received the rain! The Spirit has come, and the trees are now beginning to produce fruit. What else does this say? It says your threshing will continue until grape harvest, and the grape harvest will continue until planting, that's year-round production. When I give you the rain, when I give you the Spirit, you will begin producing fruit year-round. What a beautiful promise and blessing He gives when He gives us the Spirit, and we begin to produce fruit in the Spirit, and it's a year round thing! Then we will eat from the food and live securely in our land.

Here's what's we're talking about, when we walk by the Spirit and not by the Law, not by the flesh, not by your own efforts, but when we walk by the Spirit, we're not trying to be good people, we *ARE* good people. We do not attempt to be patient, we are patient, we are at peace. We do not present a good face from a bad heart; we are *renewed* in our hearts. We don't act nice; we are transformed into a loving person. We do not say we are good, and we walk in goodness. We do not pretend to be committed, we are committed, and we are faithful. We don't labor to stay pure, we are pure, and walk in self-control. We become loving, joy-filled people, peaceful, patient, kind, good, faithful, gentle, self-controlled children of God. We walk by the Spirit and not by the flesh.

But this only happens if we're walking by the Spirit, and we have to walk by the Spirit for this fruit to be produced. But what does it mean for us to walk by the Spirit? It means listening for every instruction from the Holy Spirit and learning from every lesson that He teaches us. It means grabbing hold of the hand that guides us and letting go of what we want in the flesh and clinging to the things of the Spirit. It means walking where every move is made, keeping the Holy Spirit in mind.

Too often the church as a whole is afraid of the Holy Spirit. They don't remember that Jesus said, I am leaving you to go and sit at the right hand of the Father to intercede for you. But the Father is sending the Holy Spirit and He will guide you into all truth. (John 16:13) And in this, there is no disrespect to Jesus, our Lord, Savior and King that we bow our knees to; but we are being led by the Holy Spirit. We want the Holy Spirit to guide us into all truth and learn every lesson He has to teach us. We want to watch Him produce His fruit in us!

Psalm 46:10:

> Cease striving and know that I am God.

Who would we be if we truly walked in the Spirit, and what power to overcome would be available to us? What strength in the storms would we have? What insight would we have as to the schemes of the enemy? What health and restoration would be available by the one who raised Jesus Christ from the dead? What influence would we have over our territory? What wisdom through inspiration would we possess? What truth would we walk in and what lies could we expose? Listen, walking in the Holy Spirit *IS* key to the successful life.

Are you tired of striving to be good? Do you know what I have found out in my 57 years? It's a never ending striving. It's a never ending striving where I condemn myself on a regular basis when I fall short of the things of the Spirit. When all I needed to learn was if I would just walk with Him, just be at peace knowing that He is guiding me, just listen to what He's instructing me to do, then I don't have to strive anymore. These things naturally come out of me. Why? Because it's not something I'm producing. It is what He is producing in me.

What is causing strife in your life? What is causing pain? What is causing depression or anxiety? These things are not of the Spirit because the Spirit offers peace. He offers us Joy. He offers us gentleness and all we have to do is submit to Him so we can walk in these beautiful things. I'm asking you to begin getting in touch with walking hand in hand with the way Jesus asked us to. If you would abide in me, I will abide in you. It's the same relationship with the Spirit. If I would be willing for the Spirit to abide in me and I in Him, joy and peace would just be a normal part of our lives because He would produce it instead of me.

My prayer for you:

Father God, we just lay ourselves in front of You and say, we want the peace and the joy and the fruits of the Spirit. We want to walk hand in hand with you, Holy Spirit. We don't want to resist you. We don't want to try on our own. We want to watch you succeed through us. We want to walk in this gentleness. We want to walk in this self-control because we're being guided by you, because we're walking with you, because we're hand-in-hand with you, because we are tired of striving on our own. Tired of trying to get it done. Tired of trying to prove to everybody that we can be nice, that we can be gentle, that we can have joy and peace. Forgive us Lord for all of the facades that we put up because we're trying to prove what we can do. Instead, Father, could we just walk with You and let You do these things in us by Your amazing Holy Spirit.

Say this out loud to Him today; I love You Holy Spirit. I want a stronger relationship today than I've ever had with You. I want to listen more closely than I ever have. I want to see from Your eyes more than I've ever seen and hear Your words more than I ever have. I want to be totally, fully submitted and connected to You so that I can see what this Joyful life is, so I can see what this confident life is, so I can walk out the things of Christ. I can't do them on my own, but You can do them through me. Take me and use me because I love You, in Jesus name, Amen!

HOLY SPIRIT PRECIPITATION

Let's talk about rain, about the latter rain and the early rain. I've entitled this chapter Holy Spirit precipitation. In Israel there is an early rain and a late rain. During the early rain you plant your crop and the early rain feeds your crop. Then as the crop grows there is a latter rain that comes. The latter rain that comes is for the purpose of ripening the crop. In other words, it has been growing, it's been nurtured, it's blooming and now it's time for it to be ripened right before it is harvested. And in Israel, the early rain actually comes in the fall of the year when you plant your crop, and the latter rain comes in the spring; it's called the spring rain or the latter rain. That seems a little off to us because we're thinking about the calendar year. But when we begin to think about planting in the fall, we have an early rain in the fall and a latter rain in the spring.

As we look through scripture, the Holy Spirit outpouring for us is compared to an early and latter rain. In other words, there was an outpouring on the earth of the Holy Spirit, and it was called the early rain. And then there is the latter rain that is yet to come. You see the spring rain comes right before the harvest. And so the harvest of souls is ahead of us, and that latter rain will come. So, there is going to be a great rain, an outpouring of the Holy Spirit that comes just prior to Jesus returning and the harvest of souls. And this great outpouring of the Spirit will come to man to prepare us for the great harvest.

So let's look at what the scripture says in Joel 2:23-24:

> So rejoice, O sons of Zion, and be glad in the Lord your God; For He has given you the early rain for *your* vindication.

So this is our first indication that He's not talking about vegetation here. He's not talking about actual crops. He says, you've been given a rain for your vindication. What is vindication? One definition of vindication is to be made righteous and justified. In other words, if somebody accused you of something and it was found out not to be true, you have been vindicated. You are righteous and justified because you received a vindication from the accusation.

So he says there is an early rain that was given to make you *righteous*. It was a *vindication*. The early rain came when Jesus came to make us righteous, right? We've been given a robe of righteousness. He has made us righteous. He has vindicated us on the cross. And then there was an outpouring of the Holy Spirit called the day of Pentecost when the Spirit came. That was the early rain. The early rain came on the day of Pentecost and then Joel 2 says:

> And He has poured down for you the rain, the early and the latter rain as before. The threshing floors will be full of grain, and the vats will overflow with the new wine and oil.

Lets look at what He's expressing now. He just said there's an early rain and there's a latter rain, and at the latter rain, your threshing floor will be full of grain. Do you remember that when Christ comes, it says He is going to separate the tares from the wheat? So, the harvest has to do with pulling in the grain and the threshing floor will be full of grain when that great harvest comes at the latter rain. But it also says that the vats will overflow with new wine and oil. Those are both symbols of Holy Spirit. In other words, at that great harvest, there will be a great presence of Holy Spirit. So when the latter rain comes, we have grain, wine and oil. Grain being the great harvest of souls and we will have a great overflowing with wine and oil, symbols of the Spirit.

Now scripturally, the day of Pentecost is shown as the early rain. We can see it in Joel 2:28-29, it says:

> It will come about after this that I will pour out My Spirit on all mankind; and your sons and your daughters

> will prophesy, your old men will dream dreams. Your young men will see visions. Even on the male and female servants I will pour out my Spirit in those days.

So that's Joel giving a prophecy of an outpouring of the Spirit. So let's figure out where that prophecy got fulfilled. If we move forward to Acts 2, on the day of Pentecost we see that Peter is up speaking, and what's happening is the Spirit has come upon them. Men are speaking in tongues and rejoicing, and every one is saying, these guys are drunk. Then Peter gets up and says, "Oh no, they're not drunk." In verse 15 it says:

> For these men are not drunk, as you suppose, for it is only the third hour of the day; but this is what was spoken of through the prophet Joel.

Notice Peter says, "this is." This is what was spoken through the prophet Joel. He is saying, what you are seeing is what Joel prophesied. In Joel 2:28-29 he said the Spirit would be poured out:

> It will come about after this that I will pour out My Spirit on all mankind; and your sons and your daughters will prophesy. Your old men will dream dreams, your young men will see visions. Even on the male and female servants, I will pour out My Spirit in those days.

So this was the early rain! Christ came for our vindication, and the early rain came. The seed was planted, Christ in the ground, and the early rain came.

The spring rain, however, is a separate rain. It's a second rain and we see it in Hosea 6:1-3:

> Come, let us return to the Lord. For he has torn us, but He will heal us; He has wounded us, but He will bandage us. He will revive us after two days; He will raise us up on the third day, that we might live before him. So let us know, let us press on to know the Lord. His going forth is as certain as the dawn; and He will

> come to us like the rain, like the spring rain watering the earth.

There's a second rain, the spring rain, and He is saying He is going to come. But I don't know if you saw the calendaring of what he just said. He just said He will revive us with a spring rain after two days, when He will raise us up so that we may live before the Lord. You and I both know that we will live before the Lord when the Lord returns, right? So there's going to be a rain that comes that allows us to live before the Lord, and it will come after two days, now watch this. How long is a day for the Lord? It's like a thousand years. So how many days ago did the first rain happen? Two thousand years ago. And Christ is coming to reign on earth for how long? A thousand years, a third day. And we will live before him in that third day.

Are you getting this? He has just told us in scripture the early rain came on the day of Pentecost and then there will be two days (2000 years). And then there will be a third day where He will come, and He will reign with us being before Him. That will be the third day (another thousand years). In other words, it is two thousand years after Pentecost and we should be expecting the latter rain where Christ comes to reign before us for a thousand years. Again, we are sitting in the moment of the latter rain. This is the time to expect the last or the latter rain to come. There will be a latter rain that comes right before the harvest of souls so that we can live before the Lord.

Now I want us to look at something in the book of Zechariah 10:1-3. We are told something interesting about this rain, specifically the second or latter rain, which is the one we're looking for right now.

> Ask rain from the Lord at the time of the spring rain.

The spring rain is right before the harvest, and we know it's time for the spring rain.

> Ask rain from the Lord at the time of the spring rain–
> The Lord who makes the storm clouds; and He will

> give them showers of rain, vegetation in the field to each man.

That "vegetation in the field to each man" is a confirmation that it is time for the harvest. The vegetation is in the field. He's saying it's time for that second rain, but I want you to ask for that second rain. Why would we be asking for rain at the time of the rain? It doesn't make sense that we should ask for something at the same time we would be expecting it. Why do I need to ask for rain if it's expected to rain at this time?

Let's look a little deeper.

> Ask rain from the Lord at the time of the spring rain– The Lord who makes the storm clouds; and He will give them showers of rain, vegetation in the field to each man. For the teraphim speak iniquity, and the diviners see lying visions and tell false dreams; they comfort in vain.

He's telling us what's going on in this time and why we should be asking for rain, even though it's the time for the rain. First, it's because the teraphim speak iniquity. So do you have teraphim speaking iniquity to you? What is a teraphim? Teraphim is a household false god. It's a god that the people were serving. It was an idol they kept in their home to serve. They bowed down before these false gods in their homes. The diviners referenced here are the false prophets; they work under a spirit of deception. They are deceived by their own lust, and the words they give are not inspired. They are lying in their visions, they tell false dreams and they comfort in vain. Why are they comforting in vain? Because what they're saying is not inspired of God. They are lying. And because these people are speaking false things,

> Therefore, the people wander like sheep. They are afflicted because there is no shepherd.

There are no true shepherds, no shepherds of God. So continuing in verse 3 God says,

> My anger is kindled against the shepherds.

The ones He is talking about are the false ones.

> And I will punish the male goats.

"Male goats" in this case is a reference to those leaders. The leaders of the people are the ones He is calling the male goats.

To review, what He has laid out here is to ask for rain at the time of the spring rain because there are false leaders, but then he says, the Lord is going to do something about this problem. This is where it gets fun.

> For the Lord of hosts has visited His flock, the house of Judah, and will make them like His majestic horse in battle.

Is that not great? So there's going to be a rain. There needs to be a harvest. There are lying people out there, and God is going to make us horses. What?

The key to understanding this is that He says He's going to make us majestic horses. A majestic horse is a title, it's a battle horse, a warrior horse. What's the difference in an average horse and a majestic horse? An average horse is skittish and runs away from the battle, but a majestic horse runs to the battle! So He says, "I'm going to make you a people who run 'to' the battle, not away from the battle!" The Lord will visit His people in the spring rain to make them run to the battle.

But what does this have to do with rain that makes us run to battle? Well, we know there's rain coming, which is the latter rain before the harvest, and 'this rain' is going to make us want to run to the enemy. What can we learn about how the latter rain accomplishes that from the first rain? Well, the first rain was at the day of Pentecost. There was a guy named Peter, and Peter was pretty skittish. Peter was a guy who denied even knowing Jesus three times, right at the moment Jesus was being taken and captured to be crucified. He's 'running away,' if you will. Peter is not a warrior, he's not a battler, he's running, and he's skittish. As a matter of fact, after the crucifixion, he goes back to the Sea of Galilee to fish. But then Pentecost happens…

The vindication of man gets taken care of in Christ on the cross. The Holy Spirit is poured out in the early rain, and then what kind of a Peter do we have? Peter is now standing in front of all of the people and saying, you just killed the Messiah! He's boldly proclaiming the word of God in front of the same people that he had just run from; he's no longer afraid. He says, beat me, whip me, that's fine, it's all good for Christ, I'm ready to endure that. He's now a majestic battle horse after that first outpouring of the rain. It's a hint as to what's going to happen in this latter rain.

Let's continue in Zechariah 10:3-4:

> For the Lord of hosts has visited His flock, the house of Judah, and will make them like His majestic horse in battle. From them…

Who's them? Judah. He just said he's going to visit Judah:

> From them will come the cornerstone.

Who's the cornerstone? Who's the lion of Judah? Jesus! So he's saying from Judah will come Jesus.

> From them the tent peg,

That's kind of a deep one, but if you look at the tent peg, it could probably mean one of two things in this case. In the time of Debra, Jael had a tent peg and she drove it through the enemy Sisera's head as he was on the ground sleeping. She actually drove it through his temple and into the ground. So with a tent peg, she defeated the enemy. Or it could mean the center post of the tent where they would hang the things that make the tent substantial.

But He says from Judah will come a tent peg, then goes on to say:

> From them the bow of battle.

Christ returns on a horse with King of Kings and Lord of Lords written on his thigh, ready to gather us together and go to Armageddon for the great battle. It goes on to say:

> From them every ruler, all of them together.

Christ has come to claim his own. We will join him in that battle in defeating the enemy. And in verse 5 it says:

> They will be as mighty men. Treading down the enemy in the mire of the streets in battle; And they will fight, for the Lord will be with them; And the riders on horses will be put to shame.

When he speaks of riders and horses here, he is not talking about majestic horses but the enemy horses, and then in verses 6 and 7:

> I will strengthen the house of Judah, And I will save the House of Joseph.

What does that mean? Judah and Joseph are actually all of Israel, with the northern and southern kingdoms combined, He is talking about all of his people together.

> And I will bring them back, Because I have had compassion on them; And they will be as though I had not rejected them. For I am the Lord their God and I will answer them. Ephraim will be like a mighty man…

Why did he mention Ephraim? We just talked about the northern and southern kingdoms being combined, so we have all of Israel together. Why do we need Ephraim in the mix separately? The name Ephraim means doubly fruitful. We're talking about the time of the harvest, and there will be a double fruitfulness.

> Ephraim will be like a mighty man, and their heart will be glad as if from wine;

Remember the words doubly fruitful? He says as if from wine, so here we go with the Holy Spirit again. Ephesians 5:18:

> Do not get drunk with wine, for that is dissipation, but be filled with the Spirit.

Remember the day of Pentecost? The people said, “it seems like they are drunk with wine.” They were not drunk with wine; they were filled with the Spirit. But back to Zechariah:

> Indeed, their children will see it and be glad, their heart will rejoice in the Lord.

Malachi 4:6 says:

> He will restore the hearts of the fathers to their children and the hearts of the children to their fathers.

In other words, the descendants will be glad because of the latter rain and because of the fight that is within them and because Christ has returned. What a glorious time!

I want to go back to the question, why do we have to ask for rain if it's the time for the rain? I think there's an answer in scripture. We just read that in Zechariah 10, but if we go forward to Zechariah 14, there's an indication of why he's telling us to ask. In Zechariah 14:17 it says:

> And it will be that whichever of the families of the earth does not go up to Jerusalem to worship the King, the Lord of hosts, there will be no rain on them.

What did he just say? He said if they want rain, they must worship the King, they must go before the King. They must enter the throne room and they must be before for the Lord of hosts. If we go before the Lord of hosts and we worship the King, then there will be rain, and if we don't, there will be no rain. What's does this mean? If we want the Holy Spirit poured out on us, we must come before Him during the time of the rain and *ask for it!*

We know this concept; we just don't know we know it. Let's look in Luke 11, which we've read many times, and could ask the same question we are asking about anything, even when God has promised us everything. Luke 11:9-10 says:

> So I say to you, ask, and it will be given to you; seek, and you will find; knock, and it will be opened to you. For everyone who asks, receives; and he who seeks, finds; and to him who knocks, it will be opened. Now suppose one of you fathers is asked by his son for a fish; he would not give him a snake instead of a fish, will he? Or if he is asked for an egg, he will not give him a scorpion, will he? If you then, being evil, know how to give good gifts to your children, how much more will your heavenly Father give the Holy Spirit to those who ask Him?

So He says to you, "ask," and it will be given to you. For everyone who "asks," receives. And he wraps the conversation up by saying, go before your heavenly Father and ask for the Spirit, and you will receive the Spirit. Even today, we are told to ask for Holy Spirit, even today in the Church Age. Even today, when the Spirit is being poured out on all mankind. Even today, when we have accepted Christ, he says ask for the Spirit and I will pour the Spirit out on you. See, God loves pouring out His Spirit on all men, on all mankind. I've taught many times that every Old Testament story is a physical representation of what we are to spiritually understand in the New Covenant. So let's go back and look at rain in the Old Covenant to see what the physical representation of the spiritual outpouring looks like.

Exodus 16:4 says:

> Then the Lord said to Moses, “Behold, I will rain bread from heaven for you.”

And Psalms 78:23-28 it says it like this:

> Yet he commanded the clouds above and opened the doors of heaven; He rained down manna upon them to eat and gave them food from heaven. Man did eat the bread of angels; He sent them food in abundance.

What is the bread of heaven for you and me? Jesus! So what is he saying? He commanded the clouds above, He opened the doors of heaven and He gave us Jesus, the bread of life. God also literally gave Him abundantly. He gave us abundant life in Christ.

> He caused the east wind to blow in the heavens and by His power He directed the south wind. When He rained meat upon them like the dust, even winged fowl like the sand of the seas, then He let them fall in the midst of the camp, Round about their dwellings.

Now what is he talking about here? He is talking about the fact that He also supplied them with food. “This is my body,” Jesus said. God supplied them with the meat and the bread. Now look at verse 29:

> So, they ate and were well filled, And their desire He gave to them.

Don't miss this. God will give you the desires of your heart. You want the new car? Ask God for it, He will give it to you, right? No! God will “give you” the desires of your heart. The desires that you have in your heart will be from God. So what were the desires that He gave them? The desire that He put in them was hunger, and then He provided the bread and the meat for them. He gave them “the desire.” We need to eat, then God said I am going to supply the manna and the quail.

Leviticus 26:3-5:

> If you walk in My statutes and keep My commandments so as to carry them out, then I shall give you rains in their season, so that the land will yield its produce and the trees of the field will bear fruit. Indeed, your threshing will last for you until grape gathering, and grape gathering will last until sowing time.

He just said, year round, I'm providing for you.

> You will thus eat your food to the full and live securely in your land.

Deuteronomy 11:13-14:

> It shall come about, if you listen obediently to my commandments which I am commanding you today, to love the Lord your God and to serve Him with all your heart and all your soul, that He will give the rain for your land in its season, the early and the late rain, that you may gather in your grain and your new wine and your oil.

We just talked about that, the early rain and the late rain, and the late rain brings a great harvest with the Holy Spirit.

So if we ask, there's an expectation that we get the rain. This is how you know it, John 7:37-39:

> Now on the last day, the great day of the feast, Jesus stood and cried out, saying, "If anyone is thirsty, let him come to Me and drink. He who believes in me, as the Scripture said, from his innermost being will flow rivers of living water. But this He spoke of the Spirit, whom those who believed in Him were to receive.

I want to look at one other thing. In the book of Zechariah 10:1 where we started:

> Ask rain from the Lord at the time of the spring rain–

I'm telling you, this is the time of the spring rain right before the great harvest, it is 2000 years after the initial rain. This is the time of this spring rain. See this:

> The Lord who makes the storm clouds; And He will give them showers of rain....

It's interesting because God's going to send this rain from a storm cloud, not from a sprinkle. A storm cloud doesn't produce sprinkles. A storm cloud produces showers. It produces a downpour. It will drench you. It will soak you to the bone and God is saying, ask for the Holy Spirit and I will utterly drench you with the Holy Spirit in the time of the rain!

So when we get drenched, we go back to what we saw in the first rain. We begin to walk in the Spirit, not in the flesh. We worship in the Spirit, not in the flesh. We begin to prophesy, we begin to speak in tongues, we begin to heal the sick. We begin to deliver those in bondage, and we begin to raise the dead. We demonstrate the power of the Holy Spirit, and we walk in victory, not defeat. We build one another up, and we bear the fruit of the Spirit. We become more than conquerors, and we share the good news of Jesus Christ with boldness and we overcome this world. When we ask for the rain, we ask for the Spirit! And here's what's really exciting to me, I don't know of any believer that doesn't think Jesus is coming back soon. Everything in scripture tells us it's almost show time, and you know what happens right before show time!? God sends the latter rain for the harvest to get it ready. And He is going to pour out His Spirit! This is what He's saying to you, are you willing to ask to be drenched by the Spirit?

My prayer for you: God, we want to run to the battle and defeat the enemy, and we want to pull in a great harvest. We want to be prepared, and God, we cannot be prepared without the rain. We cannot be ready for the time of the harvest without the rain. We need you to pour your Spirit out on us. We need you to pour your Spirit out on your people that they may prophesy, that the sick may be healed, that bondages will be broken, that salvation will be rampant, and that we would be bold in sharing the gospel of Christ in this time. We want the rain, and we're asking! We want Your Spirit poured out so that we can work in the ways that you've called us to work. Victory is ours, and we are overcomers! We are not victims in this world, so God, we call for You to pour it out! Release Your Spirit on your people; we're asking for rain at the time of the spring rain! God, bring Your rain! Bring your Rain! Bring Your Rain! God, let it Rain! God, we pray that you would pour out your rain because your people are asking for it. We love you and we thank you in Jesus name. Amen!

HOLY SPIRIT TRANSFORMATION

Lets talk about Holy Spirit transformation. How does the Holy Spirit transform us? I believe that one of the best ways to illustrate this is to go back in scripture and look at one person who was transformed by the Holy Spirit. I would first like to talk about his life prior to the Spirit. This man's name is Peter, and we have plenty to read about him in the Bible. Peter's first interaction with Jesus was on the Sea of Galilee near Capernaum, and it's recorded in Luke 5:8. He has been fishing all night and it hasn't been a productive night. Jesus comes to him and says, I want to stand in your boat and I want to preach to the people on the shore. And He does that. Then Jesus says, okay, now I want you to push out a little further and I want you to throw your nets out. And Peter's response is, we've been fishing all night and we haven't really caught anything. I'm not really excited about your request, but since you asked me to, I will. And so they throw the nets out, and when they go to bring the nets in, there are so many fish in the nets that they are literally breaking the nets. And Peter has this moment of realization that he's been fishing in this same spot and there's nothing; but when Jesus is with him, there's abundance. I want you to look at Peter's response to recognizing who he's with in Luke 5:8:

> But when Simon Peter saw that, he fell down at Jesus' feet, saying, "Go away from me Lord, for I am a sinful man!"

This is Peter at the very beginning of the conversation with Jesus and his recognition of himself is, "I am a sinful man." I just need to know, is there anyone reading this that is beating yourself up over your sin? Is there anyone that feels like you're constantly unworthy of Jesus, constantly unworthy of what God has for you? If that's the case, then what I want to say to you is that the Holy Spirit can do something about that! Because, when we go on and look at the life of Peter, there's an interaction while he's following Jesus that takes place in Mark 8:33. Peter has just done this amazing thing by professing that Jesus Christ is the Son of the living God. And Jesus goes on to explain to them something and in Mark 8:31-33 it says:

> And He began to teach them that the Son of Man must suffer many things and be rejected by the elders and the chief priests and the scribes, and be killed, and after three days rise again. And he was stating the matter plainly. And Peter took him aside and began to rebuke Him, But turning around and seeing His disciples, He (Jesus) rebuked Peter and said, "Get behind Me, Satan; for you are not setting your mind on God's interests, but man's."

I don't know about you, but I'm relating to Peter. Does your mouth often get you in trouble? Do you sometimes spout out your opinion and then realize you should not have said anything? Do you ever post something on Facebook and then have to go take it down because of what you said, and the mess it created? Do you realize on a regular basis that you keep operating in the flesh, not thinking on things from a spiritual perspective? Does it seem that you can't keep your mind on Jesus and the things of the Spirit? But instead of approaching things from a spiritual perspective, you're always trying to control them and manipulate them to what you think is right? Well, the Holy Spirit can do something about that!

Jesus has to go to the garden. He knows the crucifixion is coming and He's going there to pray. So He is in the garden of Gethsemane and He begins to pray. Then He asks Peter, would you stay here and watch? I know there are guards coming, I know I'm going to be arrested tonight, but I have to pray; I want you to stay here and watch. Matthew 26:39-41:

> And He went a little beyond them, and fell on His face and he prayed, saying, "My Father, if it is possible, let this cup pass from Me; yet not as I will, but as You will." And he came to the disciples and found them

> sleeping, and said to Peter, "So, you men could not keep watch with Me for one hour? Keep watching and praying that you may not enter into temptation; the spirit is willing, but the flesh is weak."

I don't know if you have ever been in the place where you just feel like you have let Jesus down. How about the fact that it's even in the simplest forms of obedience to Jesus you just can't handle? Like, you just see this failure point coming. You can't stay focused on what He's told you to stay focused on. I'm here to tell you, Holy Spirit can do something about that!

So, Jesus is going to be arrested and it's going to be brought before Annas and Caiaphas. And this happens in Matthew 26:51-54:

> And behold, one of those who were with Jesus (John 18:10 tells us it was Peter) reached out and drew out his sword, and struck the slave of the high priest and cut off his ear. Then Jesus said to him, "Put your sword back in its place; for all those who take up the sword shall perish by the sword. Or do you think that I could appeal to my Father, and He will at once put at My disposal more than twelve legions of angels? How then will the Scriptures be fulfilled, which say that it must happen this way?"

Can you imagine being Peter in that moment? "But I was doing that for you! I was standing up for you. I was trying to do the right thing!" And then Jesus says, put it down, you're handling this wrong. Have you ever gotten a spanking in public for doing something impulsive? Have you ever gotten yourself into a mess because you blew up when you should have actually just stayed calm? Have you ever been arrested for doing something dumb? Again, the Holy Spirit can do something about that!

If I keep looking at Peter's life, Jesus gets arrested. He's taken into Jerusalem. Peter knows there's a trial going on. And in Matthew 26:57-58 it says this:

> Those who had seized Jesus led him away to Caiaphas, the high priest, where the scribes and the elders were gathered together. But Peter was following Him at a distance as far as the courtyard of the high priest, and entered in, and sat down with the officers to see the outcome.

Then we go down to verse 69-75:

> Now Peter was sitting outside in the courtyard, and a servant-girl came to him and said, “You too were with Jesus the Galilean.” But he denied it before them all saying, “I don't know what you're talking about.” When he had gone out of the gateway, another servant-girl saw him and said to those who were there, “This man was with Jesus of Nazareth.” And again, he denied it with an oath, “I do not know the man.” A little later the bystanders came up and said to Peter, “Surely, you too are one of them; for even the way you talk gives it away.” Then he began to curse and swear, “I do not know the man!” And immediately a rooster crowed. And Peter remembered the word which Jesus had said, “Before a rooster crows, you will deny Me three times.” And he went out and he wept bitterly.

Have you ever had that moment when you realize you were supposed to stand up for your faith and you didn't or when you denied being a Christ follower by your actions? Have you ever had that moment where you were fearful of what others would think of your belief in Jesus or stuck to your guns in a lie until it was too late? That's really what Peter did. He lied, but he wouldn't even deny the lie, he wouldn't even fess up to his own lie, until it was too late. I'm here to tell you the Holy Spirit can do something about that!

This denial of Christ comes after Peter goes to the Sea of Galilee, throws a hook in the water, and brings out a fish that has money in its mouth to pay his taxes. It happens after Peter sees Jesus curse a fig tree and it withers and dies. It happens after Peter gets to walk on water, and after he gets to go to a mountain where he sees Moses,

Elijah, and Jesus glorified! This denial happens after these things happen! Peter got to see these things firsthand, and he *still* stands there and denies Christ. You and I might describe this as pathetic. How does one see the things Peter saw and then deny Christ?

But there was a moment, there was a day recorded in scripture where everything changed. This Peter we knew as the bumbler, who pops-off at the mouth, who causes problems, this Peter we know who denies Christ, changes. It all changes after this day called the day of Pentecost. On that day of Pentecost, the very breath of God blows over Peter and those in the room, and a baptism of fire comes. A baptism in the Holy Spirit comes, and this same man who failed so many times has a single experience with Holy Spirit and something dramatic changes, something drastic changes about him. Something becomes different and new about Peter from that one experience with Holy Spirit. Let me show it to you. If we go into Acts 2:14-24, which is after his interaction with the Holy Spirit. This same Peter does this in Jerusalem:

> But Peter, taking his stand with the eleven, raised his voice and declared to them.

Now watch who he's declaring to:

> "Men of Judea and all you who live in Jerusalem. let this be known to you and give heed to my words."

This was the guy who was hiding from a threat about Jesus just about a month and a half before. Now he's standing up and he's saying, everybody listen to me! Now watch what he says in 22-25:

> "Men of Israel, listen to these words: Jesus the Nazarene, a man attested to you by God with miracles and wonders and signs which God performed through Him in your midst, just as you yourselves know–this Man, delivered over by a predetermined plan and foreknowledge of God, you nailed to a cross by the hands of godless men and put Him to death. But God raised Him up again, putting an end to the agony of

> death, since it was impossible for Him to be held in its power."

Now verse 36:

> "Therefore, let all of the house of Israel know for certain that God has made Him both Lord and Christ–this Jesus whom you crucified."

Here's what I'm saying. He just stood up in front of everyone and said, I KNOW THIS JESUS! He didn't have any fear at all, but he had fear of a servant girl previously in the courtyard. She was too much for him, but now he'll stand up in front of everybody in Jerusalem and say, this man is Jesus the Messiah! He has a new boldness about him that he didn't have before. If we look in Acts 3, he is on his way to the gate. There's a man sitting there who is lame and cannot walk. Peter walks up to him and it says in Acts 3:4-7:

> But Peter, along with John, fixed his gaze on him and said, "Look at us!" And he began to give them his attention, expecting to receive something from them. But Peter said, "I do not possess silver and gold, but what I do have I give to you: In the name of Jesus Christ the Nazarene–walk!" And seizing him by the right hand, he raised him up; and immediately his feet and his ankles were strengthened.

Peter just healed a man! He just spoke into him, grabbed his hand, cured the lameness in him, and now he can walk. So let's look in Acts 4:5-10:

> On the next day, their rulers and the elders and scribes were gathered together in Jerusalem.

When was the last time Peter saw the rulers and the elders and the scribes gathered? It's called the Sanhedrin, and it was on the day that they went to try Jesus, and Peter hid! They were gathered together in Jerusalem and Annas and Caiaphas were there, the two people that made him afraid.

> And Annas the high priest was there, and Caiaphas and John and Alexander, and all who were of high-priestly descent. When they had placed them in the center, they began to inquire, "By what power, or in what name, have you done this?"

Peter, how did you heal that guy? He's speaking to the same group of people to whom he did not want to admit that he even knew Jesus. He's just healed someone. He is standing in front of these same two people and they're saying, "Peter, how did you heal this person?" And this is his response:

> Then Peter, filled with the Holy Spirit, said to them, "Rulers and the elders of the people, if we are on trial today for a benefit done to a sick man, as to how this man has been made well, let it be known to all of you and to all the people of Israel, that by the name of Jesus Christ the Nazarene, whom you crucified, whom God raised from the dead–by this name this man stands here before you in good health.

He has no fear of Annas and Caiaphas anymore! He said, you want to know how? I'll tell you how. You remember Jesus? You crucified Him, but it was Him, His power did it! Then go to Acts 5:14-16:

> And all the more believers in the Lord, multitudes of men and women, were constantly added to the number, to such an extent that they even carried out the sick into the streets and laid them on cots and pallets, so that when Peter came by at least his shadow might fall on any of them. Also the people from the cities in the vicinity of Jerusalem were coming together, bringing people who were sick or afflicted with unclean spirits, and they were all being healed.

I want you to think about what that is saying about Peter. The city is saying, get out there and get in that man's shadow and you can get healed! This is a whole different Peter than we were talking about earlier, than the one who was hiding from questions about Jesus. Acts 9:37-42 says:

> And it happened at that time that she fell sick and died; and when they had washed her body, they laid it in the upper room. Since Lydda was near Joppa, the disciples, having heard that Peter was there, sent two men to him, imploring him, "Do not delay in coming to us." So, Peter arose and went with them. When he arrived, they brought him into the upper room; and all the widows stood beside him, weeping and showing all the tunics and garments Dorcas used to make while she was with them, But Peter sent them all out and he knelt down and prayed, and turning to the body, He said, "Tabitha, arise." And she opened her eyes and when she saw Peter, she sat up. And he gave her his hand and raised her up; and calling the saints and widows, he presented her alive. It became known all over Joppa, and many believed in the Lord.

Are you hearing this? Peter just raised somebody from the dead! When he talks about the tunics and all that Dorcas made, they're talking about what they wrapped her in as burial clothes. And they were all weeping and mourning because it was over, done. Peter came in and said, get out, let me take care of this. Tabitha gets up, and he says we're going to go show them that you are now alive! Tabitha gets up, as Peter has just raised this girl from the dead!

If we go to Acts 10, he then gets a vision. Peter has a vision of a sheet coming down and there were animals on it. And the Lord says, take and eat, and he says, I can't eat, those are not clean animals. The Lord says, don't call unclean what I've called clean. I want you to go to Cornelius's house, which is Caesarea Maritime on the coastline. So, he goes there and he meets with this Roman Centurion and he says, you're a Gentile, but I'm going to tell you about Jesus. And he shares the gospel with him and the Holy Spirit falls on Cornelius and his family and everybody gets saved. So, Peter starts the whole thing of the Gentiles being grafted into the family of God!

In Acts 12, he's in prison and the scripture says an angel taps on him and says, "let's go buddy, we're walking right out of here," and he walks right out of there!

Here's what I'm saying. Look at this scenario before this experience with Holy Spirit. He's beating himself up over sin. He's getting in trouble for saying things he shouldn't say. He's letting Jesus down with even the simplest of requests. He's acting impulsive and he's living by the sword. He is in outright fear three times, denying that he even knows Jesus. Then he has this experience with Holy Spirit on the day of Pentecost, and after that experience, he's boldly speaking about Jesus! He's healing someone who is lame! He's confronting the very people he was afraid of! People just want to get near him so they can be healed! He raises someone from the dead! There's a transformation that has happened in Peter's life!

This transformation also happens to other people in scripture. We hear of a man named Steven whom the Spirit came upon in Acts 6:9-10:

> But some men from what was called the Synagogue of the Freedmen, including both Cyrenians and Alexandrians and some from Cilicia and Asia, rose up and argued with Stephen. But they were unable to cope with the wisdom and the Spirit with which he was speaking.

They were unable to cope with Stephen's wisdom because he was filled with the Spirit.

In Acts 8:4-8, there's a man named Philip.

> Therefore, those who have been scattered went about preaching the word. Philip went down to the city of Samaria and began proclaiming Christ to them. The crowds with one accord were giving attention to what was being said by Philip, as they heard and saw the signs which he was performing. For in the case of many who had unclean spirits, they were coming out of

> them shouting with a loud voice; and many who had been paralyzed and lame were healed. So there was much rejoicing in that city.

Are you hearing this? Philip had healed so many people that the entire city said, what has happened to that guy? He can heal people, so let's rejoice!

Let's look at Ananias in Acts 9:17:

> So Ananias departed and entered the house, and after laying his hands on him said, "Brother Saul, the Lord Jesus, who appeared to you on the road by which you were coming, has sent me so that you may regain your sight and be filled with the Holy Spirit."

Here's a nice guy who gets the call. Ananias, you've been filled with the Spirit, so lay hands on Saul and let him see again.

In Acts 13:9-11, that same Saul:

> But Saul, who was also known as Paul, filled with the Holy Spirit, fixed his gaze on him, and said, "You who are full of all deceit and fraud, you son of the devil, you enemy of all righteousness, will you not cease to make crooked the straight ways of the Lord? Now, behold, the hand of the Lord is upon you, and you will be blind and not see the sun for a time." And immediately a mist and a darkness fell upon him, and he went about seeking those who would lead him by the hand.

What? Filled with the Spirit, he told a man, you will no longer see, and the man goes blind!

And then 1 Corinthians 2:1-5:

> And when I came to you, brethren, I did not come with superiority of speech or of wisdom, proclaiming to you

> the testimony of God. For I determined to know nothing among you except Jesus Christ, and Him crucified. I was with you in weakness and in fear and in much trembling, and my message and my preaching were not in persuasive words of wisdom, but in demonstration of the Spirit and of power, so that your faith would not rest on the wisdom of men, but on the power of God.

Listen to what he's saying, "I didn't come to you to convince you of the Torah. I didn't come to you to explain scripture to you. I wasn't trying to get you to be a more educated, knowledgeable group. What I was trying to let you see is that there's power in the Spirit to heal and do the miraculous. I want you to see that, because then I know you will go back to the word and try to figure out this God."

I see a man named Agabus who was a prophetic man of the time, and in Acts 11:27-28 it says:

> Now at this time some prophets came down from Jerusalem to Antioch. One of them named Agabus stood up and began to indicate by the Spirit that there would certainly be a great famine all over the world. And this took place in the reign of Claudius.

He prophesied a worldwide famine and it happened. Filled with the Spirit, he could prophesy about worldwide events!

I see this kind of occurrence happened in the Old Testament too. Joshua, filled with the Spirit, leads the people of Israel. Othniel, filled with the Spirit, conquers the enemy of Mesopotamia. Gideon conquers the Midianites with torches, clay pots and horns! He just shows up filled with the Spirit, blows horns, breaks clay pots and the enemy kills themselves, that's the Holy Spirit at work! Samson, filled with the Spirit, took a lion and tore him in half; and Bezalel, filled with the Spirit, has wisdom, understanding, knowledge and craftsmanship.

What is the point, and why are we talking about this? Because in 1 Thessalonians 1:5 it says this:

> For our gospel did not come to you in word only, but also in power and in the Holy Spirit and with full conviction; just as you know what kind of men we proved to be among you for our sake.

In other words, when we see the Spirit come upon us, there will be a transformation in us, and we cannot be the same! After an interaction with the Holy Spirit, we will never be the same because when the Spirit comes upon us, He brings power, authority, the miraculous, healing, leadership, strength, wisdom and prophecy.

Listen, the Holy Spirit coming upon us is not the power to be average! It's not the power to be a victim, and it's not the power to be complacent. It's not the power to be apathetic or hidden. It's not even the power to become moralistic people, and it's not the power to just become "kind people" in our communities.

The same Spirit that raised Jesus from the dead lives in us! But this is what happens in our churches today. We say the same Spirit that raised Jesus from the dead lives in us, and we think that's a miraculous power that raised Jesus from the dead, but then we limit it to raising Jesus from the dead, and not us. I want you to hear this, because it's really important. That same Spirit was in Jesus when He righteously got angry at the money changers in the temple and when he wept in the garden over the sins of man. That same Spirit was in Him when he put mud in the eyes of the blind man and healed him and when he cast a demon out of a bent over woman. That same Spirit was in Him when he called the religious leaders of the day a brood of vipers and when he walked on the water. That same Spirit fought off the temptations of the enemy in the desert and was with Jesus when he gathered children around and said, we need to be like them. That same Spirit was working in Him when he carried a cross to go to Calvary for his own death. Why am I pointing this out? Because that same Spirit lives in us!

Let me ask this question. Is God powerful, authoritative, miraculous, loving, generous, and strong? Yes! Well then if He is, and the same Spirit of God lives in us, then why wouldn't we be the same? 2 Corinthians 3:18 says this:

> But we all, with unveiled face, *(which gets removed in Christ)* beholding as in a mirror the glory of the Lord, are being transformed into the same image from glory to glory, just as from the Lord, the Spirit.

What is this saying? When we are transformed by the Holy Spirit, we go from wimps to warriors, and from victims to victors! When we are transformed by the Holy Spirit, we go from pathetic to powerful and from stressed-out to strong! When we are transformed by the Holy Spirit, we go from helpless to healers and from confused to conquerors! When we are transformed by the Holy Spirit, we go from baffled to bold and from trials to transformation! Now that's transformation!

Church, who are we? Because it seems to me that the majority of churches today are still just a people who are in constant need of God to do something for them. That's what we often come to church looking for. Where is God, so he can fix my life? Where is God to fix my problems? Where is God to make me happy, and where is God when I need Him? The question I am asking is, "Why is this all about me?" When we are transformed, we begin to have power and boldness to speak into others' lives. We begin to have power and boldness to heal them and to cast demons out of them. That's who we are as transformed people. I'm asking, "What does the world see of the church?" I'll tell you what they see. They see a country club of people who get together and talk about how righteous they are, and now and then they feed hungry people. That's how they see us. We have a small reputation for helping people, but mostly we are known for just gathering together to talk about how God helps us. That's not who the church is supposed to be. The church is supposed to be the ones who go out to declare that the enemy is going to lose the territory to us! We are taking it back for the Kingdom of God!

God's church is supposed to be people who boldly proclaim The Word of God, who boldly offer healing, and who boldly offer deliverance. We are supposed to be a people who boldly know that there is a Kingdom of God, and it's ours, and it's time to bring others into it. Here's what I'm saying church, the very Spirit of God lives in us! The very Spirit of God is powerful and authoritative and generous and loving and strong, and He lives in us! And what lives in us should be dispensed to a hurting and dying world. They should see us as the ones who finally have it figured out, the ones who walk in strength, integrity, generosity and in healing. Church, they cannot see us anymore as a group of people who meet on Sunday in our little buildings to sing songs and cheer each other up. They must see us as a people who change the planet because of the strength we have!

My prayer for you:

Father God, we are done. Yes, we are done being good people who sing songs and hear sermons on Sundays. We are ready to be filled with Your Spirit and power to affect this world. The enemy has no authority over us. We command the enemy to be pushed out of our territory, and we will bring the people here into the full knowledge of Christ. We bring healing to them. We will bring deliverance to them. We will bring the very love and grace of God to them to heal their wounds. God, we will put them back together. We will restore them by Your power. We will breathe life into them. Because Your very Spirit dwells in us! It's who You are, so it's who we are. We draw a line today. We will no longer wait for You to teach us what you've already taught us. It is time for us to believe what You already taught us. Let your Spirit transform us in Jesus name! Amen.

ABOUT THE AUTHOR

Todd Mozingo, Senior Pastor, apostolic teacher, husband, father and grandfather.

Raised in ultra conservative church atmosphere to later being baptized in the Spirit, Todd has transitioned from one side of Christianity to the other. But the direction God gave him was to bring the two back together. The word of God and the Spirit of God must be united in the body of Christ.

In 2000, the Holy Spirit spoke to Todd and said he would leave the secular world of manufacturing management and enter the King's service. His wife had cancer and would pass on to her eternity only months after he received this word. But when the call came, he entered the King's service and got his Seminary degree. Progressing from one conservative, traditional church to another in every increasing responsibility, he was eventually the Senior Pastor of a growing conservative church. On a trip to Bogota Columbia to understand the revival happening there, the Holy Spirit radically baptized Todd with the baptism of the Holy Spirit. Rejected by his congregation, Todd started proclaiming the message of putting the word of God and the Spirit of God back together with the birth of Revive Church in Stuart, FL. Through the challenges of combining the charismatic and the conservative groups, Revive Church has become a place where Bible-based miracles, scriptural healing, word centered deliverance and salvations through the gospel of the Kingdom of God are a normal part of their church services.

Made in the USA
Monee, IL
23 November 2021